MICHELDEAN

Bishop's Wood

Ruardean

Courtfield

Lower Lydbrook

Up.' Lydbrook

lush knor

CINDERFORD

Speech Ho. Rd.

EFORD

NEWNHAM

FOREST OF DEAN

BLAKENEY

LYDNEY

G.W.R.

G.W. & M. J.R.

SEVERN

Britain's
Best Drives

At the age of 27, Richard Wilson applied to RADA and was accepted, to his utter disbelief. He has since had a long and successful acting career and is best known for his starring role as Victor Meldrew in the BBC's award-winning situation comedy *One Foot in the Grave*. He has acted on the silver screen as well as directing and performing in a number of West End productions, and most recently appeared in the BBC's fantasy drama *Merlin*.

Nigel Richardson is an award-winning travel journalist and former deputy travel editor of the *Telegraph*.

This book accompanies the BBC television series
Britain's Best Drives produced by Twofour Productions Ltd

twOfour

Britain's Best Drives

Journeys Back to the Golden Age of Motoring

**Richard Wilson
and
Nigel Richardson**

headline

First published in 2009 by
HEADLINE PUBLISHING GROUP

1

Cataloguing in Publication Data is available from the British Library

Hardback ISBN 978 0 7553 1900 8

Endpaper images © Phil Talbot/Alamy

Text images: Morris Traveller © Phil Talbot/Alamy;
Volkswagen Campervan © Motoring Picture Library/Alamy;
Triumph TR3 © Motoring Picture Library/HIP/Topfoto

Designed by Viv Mullet, The Flying Fish Studios Ltd

Typeset in Century Schoolbook by Avon DataSet Ltd,
Bidford on Avon, Warwickshire

Mapping by ML Design, London, derived from out of copyright OS 1:250,000
mapping and other sources

Photography © 2009 Twofour Productions Ltd

Printed and bound in Great Britain by Clays Ltd, St Ives plc

HEADLINE PUBLISHING GROUP
An Hachette Livre UK Company
338 Euston Road
London NW1 3BH

www.headline.co.uk
www.hachettelivre.co.uk

Contents

Foreword

ALONGSIDE THE A4086, IN THE village of Llanrug, north Wales, stands a row of rusting, derelict petrol pumps that look at least half a century old. The sight of them triggers happy memories in car drivers of a certain vintage. A garage, in the 1950s, was an oasis of civilisation on the wild and windy highway. It didn't merely sell fuel – measured in gallons, naturally, and personally dispensed by an attendant. Kitted out in crisp brown overalls, said attendant would also check your water and oil levels, inspecting the dipstick with a professorial air, sponge the insects off your windscreen, sew your jacket button back on, and send you on your way with a cheery wave. Nowadays you pull into a multi-functional road mall, fill up under the impatient eye of the driver behind you, and pass a PIN terminal over to a bloke who hardly raises his head from the magazine he's looking at – except to tell you, with an air of satisfaction, that your card has been rejected.

Ah, the 1950s. They really were the best decade in which to own and drive a car in Britain – weren't they? The truth is that few of us remember the reality – the mechanical unreliability, rudimentary comforts and relatively high accident rates. In all these areas, the experience of driving in Britain has improved immeasurably. Nevertheless, in the ways that really matter driving – sorry, 'motoring' – was the real thing then, no contest.

For a start motoring was a *novelty*. Even by the end of the 1950s, just a third of households had access to a car. And cars were *fun*. They weren't designed by computers like today's characterless and indistinguishable driving pods. They had personalities and were as comically varied as the different dog breeds at Crufts. Think of the Sunbeam Rapier convertible, whitewall-tyred and slightly spivvy, with a touch of Private Walker in *Dad's Army*; or the Austin A35, a painfully shy little saloon that wouldn't say boo to a mouse, let alone a goose. They were made of proper materials, like leather and wood, not plastic and velour (even if they are fire-retardant), and smelt pleasantly of hide and baccy.

A car was a doted-on companion, as frequently polished as driven, and motoring was *innocent*. We had no thought for the finite nature of the earth's resources, nor the damage that was being stored up by burning them in our car engines. Now we know we have sold our souls to the devil that is the combustion engine. We continue to drive, but it has become a not-entirely-respectable activity in which we mentally tot up the carbon we must be emitting into Planet Pressure Cooker each time we take the car out. Enjoyable? Hardly.

Motoring also bestowed *freedom* back then. In the 1950s, the decade before cheap charter flights revolutionised holidays, the car represented a new and highly individualised form of leisure that didn't rely on the mass outing by charabanc or train. You could customise your own itinerary and stop where you pleased – a convenient option when you'd been on the sauce all day at Skeggy (breathalyser testing wasn't introduced on British roads until 1967).

Finally, motoring was an *adventure*. People got about much less in those days – even vicariously, as we do today, via high definition widescreen images in the corner of the living room. Much of their own country was to all intents and purposes a foreign land. 'It is probably still true, in spite of the great increase in motoring, that few people have a really intimate knowledge of more than a strictly limited area,' wrote Christopher Trent in one of the most popular guidebooks of the decade, *Motoring Holidays in Britain*, published in 1959.

A great wodge of motoring guides was published in the 1950s, recommending different itineraries and places to stay and even offering useful nuggets of 'driving philosophy' such as this gem from *Car Driving in Two Weeks* by Lawrence Nathan, published in 1956: 'Everyone on the road, including pedestrians, is mentally deficient, therefore it all depends on you.'

A belated addition to that wodge of motoring books, *Britain's Best Drives* takes half a dozen of the most popular routes recommended in the 1950s literature and roadtests them today in a series of iconic cars of the period. The blessed intervention of synchromesh came too late for our classic fleet, so bear with us when we get the double declutching wrong and make some blood-curdling crunches down into first. Otherwise, the results are a revelation. Yes, driving in Britain has changed hugely over the intervening half-century. There were 5.7 million cars on British roads by the end of the 1950s compared to nearly 30 million now. The first stretch of motorway, just over eight miles, was opened in 1958; now there are more than 2,000 miles of blue-signed, multi-laned fast track. But away from the congestion and rude gestures that are part and parcel of driving in and around our major conurbations, Britain's roads – and the people you meet along the way – offer an insight into ways of life and thinking that have changed less than you may imagine.

From the westernmost edge of Cornwall to The Trossachs of the Central Highlands of Scotland, we drive through some of the most beautiful landscapes in Britain. Each has a fascinating story to tell of how it has been shaped by tourism, industry, literature and even television, while the people we run into are as varied, resourceful and extraordinary as only 'ordinary' people can be.

So what are we waiting for? The tank is full, the oil checked and the water topped up. Pull on the string-backed gloves. Pack the Thermos and get the old cloth maps from the glovebox. Let's get motoring.

Richard Wilson and
Nigel Richardson

Chapter 1

The North Yorkshire Moors

Scarborough – A171 to Scalby – unclassified road to Hackness and Langdale End – Dalby Forest Drive – unclassified road to A169 – A169 north, turning on to unclassified road for Goathland – back to A169, to Whitby

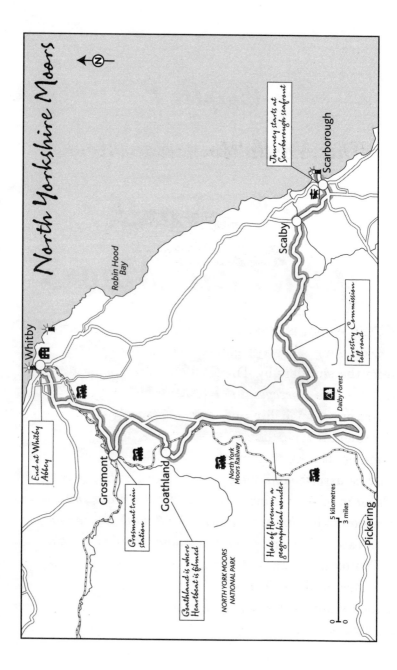

North Yorkshire Moors

Journey starts at Scarborough seafront

Scarborough

Scalby

Robin Hood Bay

Whitby

End at Whitby Abbey

Grosmont

Grosmont train station

Goathland

Goathland is where Heartbeat is filmed

North York Moors Railway

NORTH YORK MOORS NATIONAL PARK

Hole of Horcum, a geographical wonder

Forestry Commission toll road

Dalby Forest

Pickering

0   5 kilometres
0   3 miles

The North Yorkshire Moors

THE WOODY IS PARKED UP on the Scarborough seafront, drawing sideways glances and grins of recognition from the shufflers-by. The Spanish have their *paseo*, the Italians the *passeggiata* – the parade of fine clothes, social one-upmanship and coded courting by which your Continental types like to see and be seen in the cool of evening. The British, on the other hand, have what can only be described as their *potter*. And it doesn't even take place in the evening – much too parky for that in Scarborough. No, any time will do, so long as the tea stalls are still open for a cuppa and a Custard Cream.

The elderly men and women making eye contact with the Morris Minor Traveller on this autumn morning of golden sunlight are a jolly procession of bald pates and elasticated slacks. Many of these same men and women first came here 50 years ago, when the distinctive timber-framed estate car affectionately known as the Woody was still tumbling off the production line at Morris's Cowley plant. 'On weekdays as well as at weekends streams of motor coaches pour into [Scarborough] from the towns of industrial Yorkshire, disgorging some thousands of trippers near the beach, while trains arrive every few minutes packed to the doors with excursionists from even farther afield,' wrote Christopher Trent in *Motoring Holidays in Britain*.

These 'excursionists' were lither of limb then, of course, and not all arrived by coach or train. A minority – less than a third of households in 1960 – had cars, but everyone aspired to the freedom epitomised by ownership of even the humble Moggy, the Morris 1000, and its quaintly rustic sibling, the Traveller. But they could not have foreseen the radical changes about to be wrought on our travel and holiday habits over the next three decades. Within a radius of 80 miles of Scarborough, the coalfields of South Yorkshire and Durham, the Sheffield steel foundries, the woollen mills of the West Riding and the Tyneside shipyards employed many thousands of men and women in desperate need of an annual paddle and knees-up by the sea.

This was the era characterised by the phrase attributed to the Prime Minister, Harold Macmillan: 'You've never had it so good.' In fact, Macmillan, addressing a Conservative party meeting on 20 July 1957, had said: 'Go around the country, go to the industrial towns, go to the farms and you will see a state of prosperity such as we have never had in my lifetime – nor indeed in the history of this country. Indeed, let us be frank about it – most of our people have never had it so good.' Following the rationing and austerity of the late 1940s and early 1950s, as the country picked itself up after the war, the steel, coal and car industries were booming, the economy was buoyant and people were determined to spend their new-found, modest wealth on enjoying their leisure time.

Let's step on the gas and motor non-stop to the twenty-first century. And the people are back, fuller of waistline, thinner of hair and chastened by change. That job for life down the pit? It went west in 1984. The house up on the cliffs we went to every year, where the family would decant into the back rooms for the holiday season and let us live in the front (the old lady made a mean Brown Windsor soup)? No idea: we stopped taking our annual holiday in Scarborough in 1966. A week in Tenerife with Freddie Laker was just as cheap.

We're a four-car family now, if you count the grandkids, but we left the Daewoo at home for this trip down memory lane, what with the cost of petrol and the parking fees – it's pay-and-display all the way these days. No, we came by coach – like we did 50 years ago. Mind you, seeing that old Woody – isn't it in grand nick? – reminded me of the summer of 1959, when we'd just got our first Moggy and we only used it on special occasions. We'd take it for a spin, polish it till it shone and put it back in the garage – and the kids would stand on tiptoe to stare

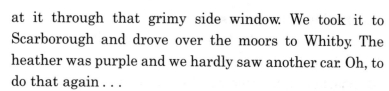

at it through that grimy side window. We took it to Scarborough and drove over the moors to Whitby. The heather was purple and we hardly saw another car. Oh, to do that again . . .

Presently we will indeed recreate that journey of half a century and nearly a lifetime ago. But first let's wander awhile on Scarborough's seafront, where the buildings and topography encapsulate the entire development of leisure and holidays in Britain. For Scarborough, you see, was what the Victorian guidebooks called the Queen of Seaside Watering Places – and, bless her calico bonnet, she still is.

Back in the early seventeenth century, only the wealthy had the time and money for leisure and they wouldn't have been seen dead at the seaside. The light and air would combine to turn fashionably pale complexions a then unfashionable brown and the assorted cutthroats, smugglers and fisherfolk who lived on this margin of land and sea would have the coat off your back in the flash of an earring. The nobs went instead to spa towns such as Harrogate or Buxton, where one drank and bathed in revivifying mineral waters whilst bemoaning the price of peacock feathers for one's hat. Then spring waters were discovered at the south end of South Bay in Scarborough, and when, in 1660, a Robert Wittie – a medical doctor with a flair for marketing – declared this particular H_2O to be a 'most sovereign remedy against Hypochondriach Melancholly and windiness', Scarborough's fame and wealth were assured. After all, where else could you get your plumbing and head sorted at the same time and go for a donkey ride on the beach afterwards?

Thus, by default, the spa-goers discovered the seaside, and Scarborough became Britain's first resort. A succession of pump houses, pavilions and bandstands were built and rebuilt on the spa site. Italianate gardens and grand villas were laid out along the cliffs above. And a bridge was built to link the spa with the town. This was certainly a grand destination – though never, perhaps, quite as exclusive as it wanted to be. For Scarborough had aspirations that were destined to fall slightly short.

This gap between seeming and being is brilliantly illustrated by the story behind the huge canvas that hangs in a corridor of the town hall. Entitled *Scarborough Spa Promenade*, it shows the Prince of Wales, the future Edward VII, and his wife at the spa in 1870. Around them swirl a host of Victorian dignitaries, taking the air and eyeing each other up. Alongside the painting, a key identifies all 82 of the lords and ladies depicted, from J. P. Petrocokino Esquire of Bradford to 'The Ladies Duncombe' (provenance unstated). In fact, the event shown in the painting never happened and was a pure money-making invention by the artist, Thomas Jones Barker. He charged local social climbers to be painted into the picture – the nearer they appeared to the Prince of Wales, the more they had to pay. It seems the craving for celebrity is hardly a recent phenomenon, but the story also shows that Scarborough was never quite as posh as it liked to think.

By the time that this imaginary event took place, the second of Scarborough's iconic buildings (the first being the Spa) had sprung up on South Bay – the vast and heavy-looking Grand Hotel, which still squats like an engine block on the sloping chassis of the foreshore. The Grand, as a blue plaque on one of its outside walls reminds us, was 'Once Europe's largest hotel', a confection of balustrades and ballrooms, of colonnades and caryatids, built to the proportions of an ocean liner. With typical Victorian pomp and vigour, it was said to have been conceived by the architect Cuthbert Brodrick on the theme of time, with 365 rooms, 52 chimneys, 12 floors and so on (though the reality doesn't quite work out that way).

The inaugural banquet in July 1867 featured a pompous French menu – *Pavise de Gibier*, anyone? – and by the early years of the twentieth century Scarborough Corporation was worried that the town's reputation for exclusivity would put off the lower orders from coming. A local guidebook writer even pointed out that frock coats were not *de rigueur*. This anonymous champion of the hoi polloi would be gratified by the changes that have taken place over the past century.

By 1950 – when the charge for an overnight stay with breakfast was 21 shillings (£1.05) – the Grand had moved with the times to the extent of allowing those men who had mislaid their dinner jackets to wear lounge suits. Churchill stayed in Room 140 several times, betraying a suspiciously Continental concept of hygiene when he asked for a bidet to be installed. But by the mid-1960s –

as Britain hitched a lift to the hotspots with Freddie Laker and co. – the place was on its uppers. It was even owned by Butlins for a while. In 2008, the Grand looks as grand as ever – from a distance. Then you notice the posters in the windows advertising 'The Great British meal offer – £3.95' and 'Nightly entertainment with visiting artiste – only £5 per person'.

The lobby, with its colonnades and balconies and vast sweeping staircase, retains vestiges of that old glory, but then you notice, parked in discreet corners, the wheelchairs and mobility scooters. This is a budget-priced rooming house for frugal pensioners who arrive in coach parties, reminiscing about their visits to Scarborough in the 1950s, when they wouldn't have dared get within 50 feet of those marble entrance pillars. Signs advertise bingo and quiz nights. A bulletin board details that day's coach outings to Goathland and Whitby or Beverley and Bridlington.

The current owners of the Grand, Britannia Hotels, are in the process of a £7 million refurbishment 'to bring the Grand Hotel Scarborough back to its former glory'. But that surely is an impossible aim, for tourism has been democratised since Cuthbert Brodrick dreamed up his time machine in brick and marble, and Scarborough is more cheerfully accessible than almost anywhere else in Britain bar Blackpool. The spa closed off its waters between the wars and no longer entertains grand ladies in crinolines. Reminding us that there is an entertainment hinterland beyond television, it showcases singers and comics with names you haven't heard mentioned for a decade or more, though it also, in a touching link with the past, continues to put on the 'legendary' Scarborough Spa Orchestra, which has been going since 1912.

If the seaside resort, as we think of it today, started in Scarborough, you could also say that it is destined to end here. For as the global economy takes a turn for the worse, and international flights – on the scale and frequency we have been taking them – become less afford-able and more environmentally unacceptable, it is to places like Scarborough that we will return. We are doing so already. In the welter of statistics generated by tour-ism, Scarborough ranks third in Britain (after London and Blackpool) for the 'annual number of overnight stays'. Six million people come here every year, spending £460 million in the process, and in 2008 the town won the government-sponsored Enterprising Britain Award for its success in transforming the social and economic prospects of the area. The old Queen of Seaside Watering Places may now ride a beach donkey instead of an elegant grey, but she still has a sizeable wad tucked in her reticule.

Aye, and she's still an eye-catcher with superb bone structure. The town consists of two sandy bays scooped as cleanly as ice cream from the North Sea coastline and divided by the wooded and battlemented prow of Castle Hill. North Bay, with nothing visible bar sand and gardens, has, amazingly, resisted the depredations of development. South Bay, which has the Spa and the

Grand, was likened in an 1889 guidebook of *Seaside Watering Places* to the Bay of Naples.

'See Scarborough and die' doesn't have quite the same ring to it but the Bay is dazzling on a sunny morning. Light bounces off its waters and at low tide, with the sand stretching like glass to the distant waterline, backlights the handful of dog walkers, turning them into stick-like silhouettes.

Catching up with that group of potterers who have just smiled at the Woody, we find they are in line with Jimmy Corrigan's amusement arcade, on the beach side of Foreshore Road, watching something taking place at the edge of the sand, just beyond the railings. A sand sculptor called Stephen Mason – who belongs to a noble Scarborough tradition of sand sculptors – is busy making a dinosaur, using as reference a children's picture book. 'It's a diplodocus,' he says. 'The best I can do out of sand anyway.'

We turn and contemplate the seafront amusements – Terror Tower ('Tour the film sets of the chiller movies'), the Virtual Explorer flight simulator, John Bull, the rock-maker – then amble on to the gloriously kitsch Harbour Bar on Sandside, an ice-cream parlour in Formica and neon that looks very rock 'n' roll, very 1950s, but in fact dates from 1945. In that final year of the Second World War, a time of euphoria, uncertainty and change, Giulian Alonzi's Harbour Bar must have looked like the future – bright, healthy, casual and youthful – in which we would float to heaven on a sea of knickerbocker and pineapple glories. 'A milkshake gives double nutrition – milk and ice cream,' says a cheery slogan. 'Freshly made ice cream – always good, good all ways!' says another. Now – in an age of bookish coffee bars and fat-free dairy products – it looks like the past.

We emerge, half-guiltily, with mouths rimmed in red and yellow, and turn up Eastborough, the street which twists and climbs sharply from the seafront. Didn't there used to be a pawnbroker's here? The tattoo parlours and clairvoyants are still there, and now there are cafés offering 'OAP specials' and joke shops selling 'horror rats', male stripper sets and 'turds of all sizes'. There is also, near the top of Eastborough, a strange pastiche of Scarborough's heyday. 'Have your photograph taken in period costume,' exhorts the slogan above a replica Edwardian photographic studio, which offers to take your picture against a choice of backdrops. 'Picture yourself on board the *Titanic*,' says the sign, adding: 'Costumes slip over your own clothes.' But there is no magnificently moustached photographer who delves his head inside a velvet drape and asks you to hold dead still. There is no puff of smoke as the flash ignites. 'It's all digital,' says the owner. 'Ready in ten minutes. That's what the punters want.'

What *these* punters want is to take the Woody for a spin, so we return to the seafront, pile aboard and head out on Marine Drive, the road around the castle foreshore linking North and South Bays. Above the empty sands of North Bay, wedged among the avenues and drives where the landladies of the 1950s would ask to see couples' marriage certificates, is a Scarborough institution: the green glen of Peasholm Park. Everyone went to Peasholm Park, with its rare trees and babbling brook and boating lake with an island in the middle. They took rowing boats on the lake, watched firework displays, plotted how to smuggle boyfriends or girlfriends past the pinafored battleaxes who ran the boarding houses, and cheered while we won the war – not once, but repeatedly (three times a week in high season).

Since 1927, the lake at Peasholm Park has been the venue for 'Naval Warfare' re-enactments using electric-powered, 20-foot-long model warships steered by council employees. Between the wars, the ships were replicas of First World War vessels. After the Second World War, the template for these pretend engagements of smoke and noise became the 1939 Battle of the River Plate. Thus Peasholm Park's dinky boating lake became a vast river estuary in South America where men disguised as HMSs *Ajax*, *Achilles* and *Exeter* gave the what for to another man concealed in a model of the German pocket battleship *Graf Spee*. This is a notion of fun so loveably creaky and British that Peasholm's Naval Warfare entertainments have survived – though nowadays the 'enemy' is no longer our close and trusted European ally Germany, but a vague and unnamed Johnny Foreigner.

Having saluted the vanquishing of the foe and the raising of the Union flag, we traipse back down to Royal Albert Drive and climb back aboard the Traveller.

'Makes you proud to be British,' says one passer-by.

'That naval victory against all the odds?' says another.

'No, the car, the car. After all these years. Starts sweet as a nut.'

And she does. The Morris Minor was a design classic, the British equivalent of the VW Beetle in its simplicity, versatility, longevity and sheer charm. The original Moggy, designed by the man who would bring us the Mini, Alec Issigonis, appeared in 1948 and underwent several subsequent modifications and upgrades before production ceased in 1970. An estate version, the Traveller, with its external wooden frame, was introduced in 1953 and continued to be manufactured until 1971, by which time nearly 1.5 million Moggies and Woodies had been let loose on the world.

It was, like the Beetle, the car of the people. In 1958, a brand new Traveller cost £708 12s (an Aston Martin DB Mark III convertible retailed at £3,451 7s) and by the 1960s nearly every family in the country had some sort of connection with a Morris 1000 – its reliability made it the car of choice among commercial travellers and if you yourself didn't own one then your brother or auntie or grandfather almost certainly did. But it wasn't just its affordability, excellent handling, economical fuel con-sumption, roominess and ease of repair that made the Morris Minor so popular. Like all great designs, she seemed to take on a personality of her own. This was reflected in the nickname Moggy, one you would give to a much-loved, fleabitten old cat.

Everyone loved the Morris 1000, which meant that everyone – young, old, man or woman – was a potential purchaser. An advertisement for the Traveller from the 1950s shows, in addition to the vehicle itself, a young couple in a happy clinch with the slogan: 'Because it's so versatile. Together you'll choose the Morris Minor 1000 Traveller.' All of which makes her, well, sweet as a nut to drive. And today she may as well be called a Time Traveller, for the byways we are taking her down really do generate a sense of how motoring must have been half a century ago.

Uniquely among all the drives in this book, you would not take this road for any other reason than to enjoy it, as it doesn't really go anywhere. If you wished, for example, to drive from Scarborough to Whitby (the beginning and end of this first journey) in as efficient a manner as possible, you would not do it this way. Thus every vehicle you meet on the way – and there really aren't many – is there to enjoy the scenery and the unaccustomed pleasure of driving slowly and with consideration for other road users, whilst admiring the sylvan beauty of the surrounding forest.

The route out of Scarborough starts inauspiciously enough. From the northern suburb of Scalby we take a left turn by a stone house with an octagonal turret, following signs for 'Hackness' and 'National Park'. Past St Lawrence's Church we turn right at the T-junction and continue past a convalescent home for the National Union of Mineworkers on the left. At this point we are mired in bungaloid suburbia, but beyond the sign for the North York Moors National Park we shake off the present and enter a bucolic landscape, climbing steadily through a tunnel of broadleaf trees. Sunlight filters through the branches, casting bars of shadow across the road which rises and falls, twists and turns. The iron signposts are painted in black and white hoops. A golden labrador is sunning itself on a grass verge outside a farmyard. There are walkers on the road with poles and daypacks and, unusually, there is a rapport between them and the dreaded motor car that breasts the hill to intrude on their peace and quiet. They stand aside to let us pass and they wave an acknowledgement of our courtesy in slowing down, as well, perhaps, as a salutation to an old and much-missed friend, the Woody.

Now we descend again into woodland, past a cottage with embroidered wooden eaves, to follow the high wall of a private estate, Hackness Hall. Flowers peep over the tops of the old stone walls as we follow the 90 degree left turn of the perimeter of the estate, and presently a brown sign appears for 'Dalby Forest Drive'. Dalby Forest, on the southern edge of the North York Moors National Park, is 8,000 acres of managed woodland covering a series of criss-crossing valleys through which the road winds like a shaggy-dog story, in no hurry to come to an end.

The trees are mostly the sitka spruce, which you could call the arboreal equivalent of the Morris Minor, except that it is hardly a well-loved tree species. But this native of the west coast of North America is versatile and ubiquitous. In every landscape that we will drive through – bar Cornwall – the sitka spruce puts in an appearance, cloaking the hillsides in drab blankets and creating snaggle-toothed silhouettes of high ridges. In one of its many guises it even wheedles its way into our houses, for the white wood of the sitka spruce makes particularly good paper – perhaps for this very book.

Fortunately, Dalby Forest is not a monoculture of spruces. The symbol for the Dalby Forest Drive on the brown road signs is a conifer entwined with a broadleaf tree, and there are plenty of oaks, beeches, hazels and ashes. The wood of the latter, a tall and graceful native tree, is a natural shock absorber, which makes it good for the handles of axes and spades, for hockey sticks and rackets – and for the external half-timbering of our Woody.

On we trundle, shifting comfortably between second and third as the road rises and falls between high hedge-rows with views ahead of a hillside of melded greens – darkly coniferous and brightly broadleaf – and a jagged ridge line. Sheep graze on hillside meadows to the right, hay is baled into cylinders in stubbly fields to the left. The road narrows and the white lines disappear from the middle as we descend into Langdale End and find a pleasing conjunction of old England. There is a red postbox, and a tiny Methodist chapel rubs mutually disapproving shoulders with the Moorcock Inn, which has a sign dating from the early twentieth century: 'Ada Martindale. 6 days only. Licensed Retailer of Foreign &

British Spirits, Wines, Ales & Tobacco'. And parked outside the inn happens to be an Austin A35 – think Moggy without the charisma, though this workhorse from the 1950s and 1960s did recently achieve a measure of belated cult status when a van version was used in the Wallace and Gromit animated film, *The Curse of the Were-Rabbit*, in which Gromit drove it at daredevil speed, activating a variety of James Bond-like gadgets. The Morris 1000, of course, would not stoop to such blatant showboating.

This remote forest valley seems to be something of a spiritual hotspot, for after the Methodist chapel we pass the church of St Peter's (C of E, the faith equivalent of the Moggy) and then some yellow crosses of the religious sort begin to appear on the trunks of trees in the woodland to the left of the road. They guide us down a steep hill, where much Gromit-like blinking and rubbing of eyes ensues, for standing at the side of the road, apparently talking to sheep in a field, is a figure in a long black cloak with a distinguished beard. No, it is not the ghost of motoring holidays past, returned to guide us safely through the forest. But it is someone almost as unlikely – an Egyptian monk of the Coptic Orthodox Church. This is the principal Christian church of Egypt, where there are several million members, with a further million in different parts of the world – including, since 2004, Langdale End in North Yorkshire.

Father Bischoi, who tends sheep and makes stained-glass windows, is one of the three monks living in St

Athanasius Monastery, an early twentieth-century house tucked in the valley behind us. The house has always had religious associations – it was built as a summer retreat for the wife of devout Quaker John Wilhelm Rowntree, of the Rowntree chocolate and confectionery dynasty. Now one of its downstairs rooms has been turned into the 'church', its walls painted with icons, its ceiling with a starry sky, and there is a shelf of holy relics wrapped in sausage-shaped velvet cases. Monasticism – the practice of hiding yourself away from the bustle of the every day for the purpose of religious or spiritual contemplation and growing your own vegetables – started in Egypt in the third century AD and the first monk, St Anthony, was a follower of the Coptic sect. He said: 'Whoever sits in solitude and is quiet has escaped from three wars: hearing, speaking, and seeing. Yet against one thing he must constantly battle: his own heart.' This site was chosen, says Father Bischoi, because 'it must be a quiet place, far from the transport. The building is suitable for the peace and quiet of the monks. After we have prayer at six o'clock, sometimes we go walking in the landscape. It's fantastic.'

Leaving the monk to interrogate his own heart, we cross a narrow bridge with iron railings and pass a Forestry Commission sign that says 'North Riding Forest Park' as the limbs of Christmas tree conifers – the Norway spruce – bend like flexed biceps along the edge of the road. The Dalby Forest Drive is signposted sharp left: the village of Low Dalby is nine miles, Scarborough nine-and-a-half miles behind us. Just beyond a red telephone box, a pub table has been left at the side of the road with an honesty box and lots of jars and bags on it. The local farmer is selling pumpkin chutney, tomato relish, lemon marmalade and red cabbage for £2 a jar; fresh scones and rabbit hay are both £1 a bag. Would a Woody driver, of all people, trouser a jar of chutney without paying for it? Certainly not. And so we proceed, poorer in pocket but richer in homemade comestibles, across a dish-shaped valley to the second of our moral dilemmas: the Forest Drive toll point. Today it is unmanned, but there is a ticket machine. It is going to cost £7 – ouch! – to drive the next nine miles, but do we even hesitate? This is beginning to feel like John Bunyan's allegorical journey of tested faith, *The Pilgrim's Progress.*

The Forest Drive swoops and bends through deep woodland, delivering that sense of motoring as it used to be – or how we imagine it used to be – when fewer cars were on the road, engines were less powerful and drivers were not prone to boiling over like radiators in summer traffic jams at the least hint of delay. Without even referring to the speedo, we keep comfortably within the 30mph speed limit – to go faster would simply have the drive end sooner than it needs to – and after a while a pleasing absence becomes apparent: the absence of road markings and obtrusive road signs. Driving suddenly feels gloriously uninhibited and instinctive, as if this were an automotive naturist park. And, tootling along on traffic-free, unmarked tarmac, we slip into a reverie of an *annus mirabilis* of British motoring: 1958.

Just a year before, the outlook had been grim. The national humiliation of the Suez crisis, resulting in fuel rationing, the cost of petrol rising to over six shillings (30p) a gallon and a credit squeeze (sound familiar?) had caused a recession in the domestic car industry, much to the glee of foreign competitors. 'British manufacturers were told that their cars were outdated in appearance, lacked modern styling, were not large enough, not small enough, or had their engines in the wrong place,' reported the *Daily Mail Motoring Guide* of 1958. But what did the foreign competition know? They'd be trying to sell us Japanese cars next ... In fact, 'a miraculous change of fortune' was in the air. 'All the largest manufacturers gave their various models a "face-lift" with improved outline, wider choice of colour schemes, and more powerful engines', with no increase in prices – and Britain regained its former position as the world's largest exporter of motor vehicles. 'The motor car is no longer a luxury,' concluded the *Guide*. 'It is now regarded as an essential part of modern life.' But amid the self-congratulations, a significant event went unnoticed: Toyota exported the first Japanese car to the United States and set up an office there.

The back of the *Guide* was filled with advertisements for absurd 'motoring aids' such as the Tudor picnic chair ('will seat the heaviest person in comfort and without collapsing'), the Reversalarm ('designed to take the guesswork out of reversing') and Karspex ('the positive answer to headlight dazzle'), a pair of which we could really do with, as we endure a slightly troubling few minutes. Sunlight filtered twice – by the tree line on the high ridges and again by the branches at the side of the road – flickers across the car in a strobe effect and it is a relief to leave the trees behind. Exiting the forest, the heathery head of the North York Moors pokes above the horizon in front of us and we hit a T-junction: Thornton-le-Dale is a mile-and-a-half to the left, Whitby 19 to the right, which is the north.

The Forest Drive proper may be finished, but the unclassified road we are now on – running due north and dotted with squashed pheasants and signs for horse manure – is similarly quiet and unhurried. It's only when we hit the A169 at the Fox and Rabbit Inn that we feel we have rejoined the twenty-first century. Suddenly it's a struggle to find a gap in the traffic so that we can turn right and join the flow on this busy moorland road between Pickering and Whitby.

'Severe gradients over next 12 miles. Check your brakes,' says a blue sign. The road rises, falls and twists and there are dangerous hidden dips in which an oncoming car can easily lurk unseen for a critical second or two as you think of overtaking. Not, of course, that we do; acceleration is not the forte of the Traveller, which does 0–60 in about three days. The skies are big and sun-rinsed. In a field alongside the road, hay bales squeezed into shiny black plastic look like giant roulette balls. And here is the roulette wheel to toss them into: the Hole of Horcum.

On the map, the road does a strange thing at this point. It curves and cuts back on itself like a pair of pursed lips. In fact, it is following the rim of the Hole of Horcum, some 400 feet deep and more than half a mile across, one of those natural features usually described as an 'amphitheatre' that looks as if a giant stooped and scooped up a million tons of earth. There is, inevitably, an attendant legend about a giant doing just that – the earth he dislodged fell to form the peak of Blakely Topping a couple of miles to the east.

The A169 runs round the north-eastern rim of the Hole, then plunges away down the S bend of Saltergate Bank. A little way beyond is the first view of RAF Fylingdales, a ballistic missiles early-warning station that for many years provided such a distinctive skyline to the moors here. From the height of the Cold War in 1963, three radar installations disguised as huge golf balls flapped their ears in the direction of the Soviet Union. So surreal was the spectacle of those vast white spheres amid the wind-blasted purple and brown moorland that they became a tourist attraction in their own right. They were replaced by a single, much more boring-looking pyramid in 1992, but a slightly sinister air still pervades the place. 'This is a prohibited place within the meaning of the Official Secrets Act' warns a sign, and brightly checkered security vehicles patrol the vicinity. As we pass, a pair of undipped headlights stares at our Traveller like a hungry attack dog at a cat.

The sense of menace generated by the Cold War never succeeded in creeping across the moors to our next destination: Aidensfield – sorry, Goathland. This moorland village, two-and-a-half miles to the west of the A169, is permanently bathed in a glow of nostalgia in which it is always the earlyish 1960s – before hippies and Vietnam – and hair is kept in place with Brylcreem. For the North York Moors is *Heartbeat* country (cue the jangling guitar of the Buddy Holly song) and Goathland, which stands in for the fictional Aidensfield, is, well, its beating heart.

Since 1992, this drama series about a village bobby has warmed our collective cockles like few other programmes. At times its ratings have even exceeded those for the national institution that is *Coronation Street.* On Sunday evenings our television screens turn into fish tanks through which wholesome policemen, loveable rogues, elegant wives, cuddly animals, classic cars, highly polished steam locomotives and jolly landlords swim with soothing gentleness. And if anyone does pull a shooter he'll be from Liverpool or London and will receive his comeuppance, never you worry.

It is easy to mock the unashamed feelgood nature of *Heartbeat*, but it does tap into a sense of loss that is commonly felt throughout the country in this troubled opening decade of the twenty-first century: the loss of community.

The series is based on the 'Constable' novels of local man Peter Walker, written under the pen name of Nicholas Rhea, who joined the police force 'at the ripe old age of 16 in 1952' and worked as an errand boy and general dogsbody in Whitby police station. After doing his National Service, he returned to the force and between 1964 and 1967 served as a bobby in the North Yorkshire village of Oswaldkirk. 'It was the tiniest place imaginable,' says Walker, who is affable and shrewd, with a youthful shock of hair. 'What would the population be? About two hundred and fifty I should think. I had eight or nine little villages on my patch and a little motorbike to get around on. The crime rate was extremely low. If you got a crime it was a sneak thief. You might get a burglary, but that wouldn't be a local. You'd be dealing with other things, such as renewing firearms certificates.'

The key to Walker's Constable novels – and the television series that Yorkshire Television developed from them and for which Walker still acts as script advisor – is that they are not police procedurals about serial killers or terrorists. They are about the everyday: teenage pregnancies, car crashes, idiotic alkies, delinquent sheep... 'Things like fatal traffic accidents, sudden deaths – it was your job to deliver the news to the relatives,' recalls Walker of his days in Whitby and Oswaldkirk. 'If somebody died in hospital and their family didn't have a telephone they would phone the local policeman and he'd have to break the news.' When dealing with minor crimes – the only sort, by and large, that were committed – he tried to avoid formal charges and sending people to court. Matters would be settled with a dose of common sense.

'The police sergeant was king of his castle,' says Walker.

In conjunction with the doctor, the vicar and the district nurse – the four foundation stones on which communities rested – there were few problems that could not be dealt with within the family, as it were. He compares this way of doing things with police practice nowadays, what he calls the 'target culture' of totted up arrests and convictions by which performance is measured. This is the centralised, bureaucratic and impersonal world from which we are grateful for temporary respite when, on Sunday nights, we huddle up on the sofa and Nick Berry starts to sing.

This sense of a better past is enhanced by *Heartbeat*'s milieu: the beautiful and timeless landscapes of the North York Moors, the purple heather and the mist that snags in its upland folds, and the burnished green and black locos and rolling stock of one of the country's most scenic old railway lines. The North York Moors Steam Railway snakes between Pickering and Whitby, leaving telltale trails of white steam in the winding valley to the west of the A169. It is so dinkily perfect, it looks like a lovingly recreated model railway – the hobby, perhaps, of the giant who scooped out the Hole of Horcum. In fact, the line no longer existed in the era in which *Heartbeat* is set. As with so many branch lines throughout the country, it fell victim to the cuts recommended in the Beeching Report of 1963 (and was revived later, as a private operation, by a group of enthusiasts). But this historical anomaly does not stop the station at Goathland/ Aidensfield playing a valuable supporting role as the scene of tearful farewells and dramatic arrivals. For many of the 'telly tourists' who flock to Goathland, the NYM railway, from Whitby or Pickering, is the perfect way to arrive. It is like starring in an episode of *Heartbeat* that is all about yourself.

We, of course, have taken the Time Traveller there. And for once the Woody is not the centre of attention. For outside the single row of shops and cafés that constitute the heart of the village are not one but two Ford Anglia 105E police patrol cars – in the livery of white and a rather wimpy shade of blue – that feature in the series. Around them swirl people. Lots and lots of people, wondering quite what to do, for there is, in truth, little to do in Goathland.

The phenomenon of *Heartbeat*'s popularity manages to be both age-old and postmodern. Since Homer's *Odyssey*, consumers of fable and fiction have been drawn to the real-life settings of made-up events. In the development of British tourism, writers – and, latterly, television producers – have played a significant role in generating interest in different parts of the country and creating quasi-fictional regions such as 'Jane Austen Country' (Hampshire), 'James Herriot Country' (the Yorkshire Dales) and 'Catherine Cookson Country' (South Tyneside). This blend of the real and the make-believe has reached curious proportions in Goathland.

The irony is that this village of handsome stone villas and lodges is a posh sort of place and only used to admit the kind of people who go there now as beaters during the shooting season. The 10,000 acres of the Goathland Estate is the largest holding of the Duchy of Lancaster. 'It's quite unlike other villages on the moors; it's always been patronised by the hunting, shooting and fishing brigade,' says Peter Walker, who, having effectively invited hordes of wandering tourists into the area, now wears a heavy disguise when he visits in case men in tweeds take pot shots at him. 'It's where your salmon fisherman would go for a quiet weekend – and it's mayhem now. Tourists wandering around wondering what to do. Because there's nothing really to do, except for the shops.'

Like Norma Desmond in *Sunset Boulevard*, 'Aidensfield' has stopped turning back into herself once filming stops. And now the two identities are perplexingly interchangeable. In the row of houses that is the whirring hub of the village there are five gift shops and three tearooms. One of the shops is called 'Aidensfield Stores, Grocers and Provision Merchants'. Postcards from the series are on sale: there's 'Dr Helen Trent' and 'PC Walker' on the back of a scooter, having just got married, and 'Oscar Blaketon' with his blue Mini. There are themed tea towels, jigsaws and fridge magnets, and, in the window of the crafts centre, an offer any sane person would have to weigh up very carefully indeed: 'Buy the *Heartbeat* melamine chopping board/trivet and small tray and get the large tray, worth £4, free.'

A sure sign that we are in a strange time warp in which the twenty-first century lies many aeons in the future is to be found in the window of another gift shop, the Village Stores and Moors Outdoors Centre, where, amazingly, there is a tableau devoted to golliwogs – scores of them, in different guises and sizes, including one three feet tall. Inadvertently, this display acts as a corrective to the mush of nostalgia that is threatening to suffocate us in Goathland. For the truth is that though there may have been a heightened sense of community in the rural Britain of the 1950s, it was always an exclusive and narrowly defined community. This was the decade of large-scale immigration from Britain's colonies, especially the Caribbean, to meet the economy's need for cheap labour. Britain liked to think of herself as a uniquely tolerant and kind society, but many immigrants were shocked by the level of abuse and prejudice meted out to them. As recently as the 1950s it was both legal and common for advertisements for rented accommodation to stipulate 'No coloureds' or 'Whites only'. Immigrants worked and lived in large cities and their descendants, by and large, still do. It is still unusual to see non-white people in many of Britain's rural towns and villages and when you continue to see window displays of golliwogs – an offensive and patronising caricature of black people that was discredited a long time ago – it's not hard to figure out why.

Despite being weighed down with memories, the Traveller eases comfortably if slowly up the 1:4 hill beyond Goathland railway station and crosses lonely moorland. The cattle grid the car rattles across just before rejoining the A169 to Whitby feels like a portal between realities – behind us, in Aidensfield/Goathland, a companionable version of the 1950s that fits many Britons' sense of national identity like a pair of old slippers, whether they were alive then or not; ahead, a road of anxious speeding cars, vans and trucks, as if no one has quite enough time any longer to complete their daily tasks. In the Woody, however, it's possible to allow the needle on the centrally mounted speedometer to flicker back to the low thirties, suddenly primed for that first enchanting glimpse of the sea – and there it is, six miles to the north, a sparkling vee of blue cradled by the mouth of the River Esk. Further north, at the steep descent of Blue Bank, the red roofs of Whitby coalesce across the shoulder-like cliffs of that river mouth – and the eye is inevitably drawn to the right, where on the eastern cliff rise the ruins of the Benedictine abbey, its nave and clerestory looking as delicate as a paper cutout against the haze of sea and sunlight.

The Woody is billeted in that increasingly rare municipal commodity, a free parking space, on the top of West Cliff. Retrieving an old paperback from the glovebox it's time to set off to explore the town – and the abbey continues to dominate the view, like an actor with particular stage presence and a corker of a backstory. Once, Whitby Abbey was indeed a great and important place, for it was here, at the Synod of AD 664, that the Celtic and Roman churches thrashed out their doctrinal differences – only for Henry VIII's dissolution mob to arrive in their size elevens in the sixteenth century and kick the place to bits. Now its old stones are clambered over by schoolkids who throw things at seagulls and try to fit themselves into the sunken body-shaped graves.

Whitby was never again so grand as in those good ol' Synod days, but for nearly a century it was incredibly smelly, a curiosity worth pointing out. Between 1753 and 1837 there were 55 Whitby-based whaling ships which patrolled the waters around Greenland, hand-harpooning 2,761 whales and bringing the carcasses back to port. Boilerhouses on the harbourside rendered the whale blubber into oil, which was used to make candles, soap, margarine and paint – hence the smell. The discovery of petroleum in the mid-nineteenth century killed the demand for whale blubber, much to the relief of the wives of the boilerhouse workers and regret of the local polecat population, which had found the air unusually bracing.

Fishing, though, remained the mainstay of the Whitby economy, especially from August to October. 'Millions of herrings are landed weekly,' wrote the anonymous author of *Seaside Watering Places*. 'The visitor should walk along the quays and observe the sale by auction, landing, salting, barrelling and despatch of the fish. When the fleet is off Whitby at night, seawards the boats with their riding lights present the appearance of a town across the sea.' Still, in 1953 a motoring guide aimed at visiting Antipodeans called *A Tour by Car Through England, Scotland and Wales* was recommending that readers 'should stay a night here, to see the great fishing fleet put to sea: it is a wonderful sight'. Now it is a pitiful sight, for fishing out of Whitby has pretty much gone the way of whaling. There are just 11 big fishing boats left and 40-odd small ones, compared to the old fleet of hundreds. 'The government's ruined the fishing industry,' says an embittered old fisherman on the quayside. 'I say *government*,' he amplifies. 'I meant bunch of ******* tossers.' In a post-industrial age of depleted resources, this will be a familiar refrain throughout our drives.

After buying a tub of whelks and saluting the men who once sailed the Atlantic peaks and valleys, let's climb back up the West Cliff. At the top we pass through the arch made of the lower jawbones of *Balaena mysticus*, the Greenland right whale or bowhead whale, on the blubber of which Whitby's wealth – and pungency – was built. We settle on a bench near the whalebones – failing to notice, for the moment, whom the bench is dedicated to – and pore over the battered paperback we pulled from the Woody's glovebox. It is Bram Stoker's gothic masterpiece, the epistolary novel *Dracula*, from which almost all other hammy horror stories are derived. Many of the fictional events it describes 'happened' here. For Whitby is *Dracula*'s Aidensfield, though helpfully Stoker allowed it to keep the same name.

In the harbour below, the ghostly Russian schooner fetched up with a corpse strapped to the ship's wheel and the deathless, bloodsucking Count Dracula disembarked, disguised as a dog (perhaps it was the smell of boiling blubber that attracted him). And, just where we sit on

West Cliff, Jonathan Harker's fiancée, Mina Murray, noticed that her friend was missing one night and set out to find her, giving Stoker's prose the perfect excuse to rev up into full-blown purple gothic:

> The clock was striking one as I was in the Crescent [just behind us], and there was not a soul in sight. I ran along the North Terrace [where we're parked], but could see no sign of the white figure which I expected. At the edge of the West Cliff above the pier I looked across the harbour to the East Cliff, in the hope or fear, I don't know which, of seeing Lucy in our favourite seat.
>
> There was a bright full moon, with heavy black, driving clouds, which threw the whole scene into a fleeting diorama of light and shade as they sailed across. For a moment or two I could see nothing, as the shadow of a cloud obscured St Mary's Church and all around it. Then as the cloud passed I could see the ruins of the abbey coming into view, and as the edge of a narrow band of light as sharp as a sword-cut moved along, the church and churchyard became gradually visible. Whatever my expectation was, it was not disappointed, for there, on our favourite seat, the silver light of the moon struck a half-reclining figure, snowy white. The coming of the cloud was too quick for me to see much, for shadow shut down on light almost immediately, but it seemed to me as though something dark stood behind the seat where

the white figure shone, and bent over it. What it was, whether man or beast, I could not tell . . .

At this point a figure dressed all in black slides silently on to the bench beside us and a coronary is only narrowly avoided. Then he opens his mouth and instead of seeing blood-flecked canines we hear the affable London tones of a website designer called Mike Edwards, who follows the music and style subculture known as goth – hence the clobber. Whitby is known both for it disproportionately large goth population and for the 'goth weekends', which attract thousands of goths from all over the country.

One would assume they are here because of the *Dracula* connection – goths being fond of songs about graveyards and dancing corpses and having a generally ghoulish sense of style – but one would be wrong. Mike, who is in his 30s, attributes the goth–Dracula axis to a 'journalistic creation', but admits that 'Goths on the whole are well-educated people. A huge amount are highly creative-based and so are appreciative of literature. I'm interested in *Dracula* because goths are slightly macabre. The music's dark, the clothing's dark, but it's tongue in cheek. Cocking a snook at the bad things of life.' However, the main reason the goth weekends – now a twice-yearly event – are held in Whitby is because the organiser used to come here on holiday.

Mike himself came here not on holiday but to change his life. He moved to Whitby from north London with his wife and young son to escape the drugs and violence that were an increasing reality in his patch of the capital and to find that elusive ideal, a real community, in which to raise a family. In his street in the capital, drug deals and running fights between rival gangs were commonplace. In Whitby, the frequency and nature of crimes are more comparable with Peter Walker's Oswaldkirk in the 1960s, to judge from stories in the local *Whitby Gazette*. Under the headline 'Firefighters call-out', the *Gazette*'s intrepid newshound reports that 'Firefighters were called to Whitby's St Peter's Road after someone raised the alarm about a bonfire on Tuesday night. But when the Whitby crew arrived at around 6.15 p.m. and investigated, they found there was nothing there at all.'

The community spirit and relative peacefulness of Whitby were thrown into sharp relief for Mike in 2007, when a 20-year-old goth called Sophie Lancaster was murdered by teenagers in Lancashire because she and her boyfriend were wearing the same kind of clothes that Mike is wearing today. The bench we are sitting on, which was paid for by goths, commemorates Sophie's life. 'From a personal point of view, Sophie's death gave me the necessary kick up the backside to make a difference. I became a school governor and I've now become a cub leader. I don't sit at home moaning about the state of the community and flick television channels. I've done something.'

Another Whitbyite who can claim that he didn't just sit around gutting fish and picking his teeth is currently standing on a plinth a few feet away, staring out over

Whitby harbour. He is made of bronze and under his left arm is tucked a rolled-up maritime chart, while in his right hand he holds a pair of compasses. Captain James Cook, one of the greatest explorers in the history of mankind, wasn't born in Whitby – that honour goes to the village of Marton near Middlesbrough – but the town justifiably claims him as its own, for it was here that he learned how to be a sailor.

He was apprenticed to a Whitby shipowning family, the Walkers (the house is now the Captain Cook Memorial Museum), and in 1747, at the age of 18, went to sea for the first time on the *Freelove*, which carried coal to London. Having learned the ropes, he joined the Royal Navy and made such an impression as a navigator and cartographer that the Admiralty chose him to lead a special mission in 1769, when the planet Venus was scheduled to pass across the face of the sun – an event known as a 'transit'. The idea was that if Venus could be seen at the same time from different places during this transit, it would be possible to work out distances between planets. Boffins from the Royal Society were loaded onto a Whitby-built collier called the *Endeavour* and Cook was given the job of sailing them to Tahiti, where they would watch the transit of Venus.

Afterwards, Cook was told to push on further south in search of a 'Southern Continent', which geographers felt certain was down there somewhere. This was the first of three exploratory voyages in which he circumnavigated the globe in both directions, exploring and charting the coasts around New Zealand and Australia, Antarctica and the South Sea islands, discovering that the fabled Southern Continent didn't exist, and generally transforming our view and knowledge of the rest of the world. He was killed on Hawaii in 1779 during his third voyage of discovery.

Captain Cook, who floated into the unknown like a spaceman into a black hole, defied the stereotype of the parochial Yorkshireman for whom nowhere is comparable to the White Rose County and consequently there is never a need to travel beyond its boundaries. In *Heartbeat*, Aidensfield is the centre of the known universe and beyond it there be monsters. But Cook dared to voyage off the edge of the charts, where there were indeed monstrous dangers – in fact, he compiled the charts as he went along, like a motorist throwing down the road in front of him. Driving our Morris 1000 Traveller to Mars would scarcely be more amazing than what Whitby's honorary hero Cook achieved. Then again, you wouldn't bet against the Woody making it.

Chapter 2

North Wales

Caernarfon – A4086 – Llanberis Pass – Pen-y-Gwryd
– A498 – Beddgelert – A4085 – Caernarfon

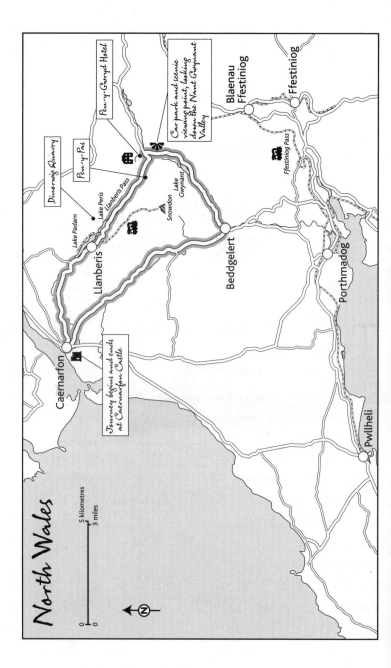

North Wales

5 kilometres
3 miles

N

Caernarfon

Journey begins and ends at Caernarfon Castle

Llanberis

Lake Padarn

Lake Peris

Llanberis Pass

Dinorwig Quarry

Pen-y-Pass

Pen-y-Gwryd Hotel

Snowdon

Lake Gwynant

Car park and scenic viewing point, looking down the Nant Gwynant Valley

Beddgelert

Ffestiniog Pass

Blaenau Ffestiniog

Ffestiniog

Porthmadog

Pwllheli

North Wales

THE MACHINES DISPENSING PARKING TICKETS are versatile and considerate – as are the banks' ATMs. They think to ask whether you would like the instructions to proceed in Welsh or English. And they do so, in the first place, in both languages. This is Caernarfon, the most Welsh of Welsh towns, and to a non-Welsh visitor it feels immediately and distinctly foreign. It is clustered with chapels and churches and the air is full of the cries of gulls and the smell of coal fires. When you walk into a shop or a pub, the chances are that the conversation you interrupt was being conducted in Welsh – and you will have understood less of it than you would a conversation stumbled upon in a remote village in South America (unless that village happened to be in Patagonia – but we'll come to that little complication). Back on the street, you notice that signs are bilingual – *Ildiwch* means 'Give way', *Dim mynediad* is 'No entry' – and instinctively you look at the number plates of cars to get some sort of take on which country you are in, only to remember with a shock that you are still in Britain. You are, to be precise, in a country within a country.

From Caernarfon, this drive takes us up into the majestic scenery on its locally quarried slate doorstep – and deep into the heart and soul of Welshness. The mountains and lakes of the area of North Wales known as Snowdonia are where the ancient people of this land retreated and consolidated when the English arrived in the thirteenth century to get them to play cricket. Within the 838 square miles of the Snowdonia National Park, 65 per cent of the population of 27,500 speak Welsh as their first language – and they still don't know a leg break from a leek.

But they do know about risking life and limb in uncommonly high and dangerous places, for this is the birthplace and home of rock climbing in Britain, where the greatest ever mountaineering feat – the first successful ascent of Everest in 1953 – was trained for. The very essence of this place – the rock beneath your climbing boots – is to be found across Britain, in our roofs and floors and tombstones. Welsh slate dressed the Industrial Revolution and the process of its removal left terrible scars on the landscape and on the population who worked it.

We must count on a particularly flash and brash motor to get us to our destination, the village of Beddgelert, in this chapter. The Ford Zodiac Mark II, which went into production in 1956 and was superseded in 1962 by the Mark III, is pure rockabilly – and not just because it hit the highway in the year in which Carl Perkins released *Blue Suede Shoes* and Elvis Presley first sang about a Heartbreak Hotel. The Zodiac, the flashier sibling of the Ford Zephyr, had a six-cylinder, 2,500cc engine, leather upholstery, streamlined transatlantic styling, a two-tone paint scheme and whitewall tyres. It also had an outrageously prominent sun visor that was the equivalent of wearing wraparound shades as well as gelling your hair up into a quiff. The overall effect was redolent of drive-in movies, and the best thing about it was that even if there wasn't a drive-in movie theatre within three thousand miles of Sheffield or Southampton, the bench front seat made the kind of activity associated with the back row of cinemas a cinch.

But let's, for the moment, leave the car – and the memories – in the car park at the foot of Caernarfon Castle and scan the awesome ramparts and polygonal towers that dwarf the town. For here is the Trojan horse at the centre of the town's Welshness – the colossal fortification built in the thirteenth century by Edward I of England after he had killed the last Welsh prince, Llywelyn ap Gruffudd. Since the invasion of 1066, the Normans had wasted little time in taking over the Saxon territories covering what is now England. But the wild lands in the far west, where they grew giant vegetables and sang in choirs, was to take another 200 years. When, after various conflicts and accommodations, the English king finally conquered the whole of Wales – this mountainous northern fastness being the last bit – Edward I wanted to make sure it stayed beaten. So he built a chain of colossal castles to encircle and subjugate the Welsh heartland of Snowdonia, of which Caernarfon Castle is the biggest – the others being Beaumaris, Conwy and Harlech.

These castles were symbols of English might – and they were also, literally, pieces of England herself in the very heart of a foreign land, where it was forbidden to speak Welsh. Edward also did a very clever thing – he stole the title of Prince of Wales for the English monarchy in order to hammer home English sovereignty. His son, the future Edward II, was born in 1284 and proclaimed the first English Prince of Wales in 1301. In 1536, during the reign of Henry VIII – ironically, a Welshman by ancestry – Welsh monoglot speakers were barred from public office and Welsh became exclusively the language of the poor and powerless. For some Welsh people – even today – Caernarfon Castle and the title of Prince of Wales are symbols of English oppression. And it does seem amazing that, despite the best efforts of the lads in white, the Welsh language has not gone the way of Cornish, but is indeed flourishing after more than 700 years of being oppressed. About a quarter of the Welsh population of three million speak Welsh today, the overwhelming majority in the north.

'It was 1282 when our last prince was killed,' says

Bethan Gwanas, a prolific author of newspaper columns, children's books and novels, who writes exclusively in Welsh. 'We have had a couple of revolts since [in particular that led by Owain Glyndwr at the beginning of the fifteenth century] but it's a long time ago. What kept Welsh alive was the chapel and the Bible – the fact the Bible was translated into Welsh so early on.'

Bethan, who's in her forties, grew up with Welsh as her first language. She thinks in Welsh, she can go for days without speaking or hearing a word of English – Welsh language television and radio stations help enormously in this respect. She wouldn't dream of speaking anything but Welsh to any of her family – though she admits that at the age of thirteen my diary was in English. Which is quite shocking now.' That's because there's always been a sense of inferiority attached to speaking Welsh.

'I was born in the sixties and you couldn't even find a birthday card in Welsh then,' she recalls. 'You were made to feel inferior, a peasant, and it all goes back to the "Treachery of the Blue Books".' This is the way the Welsh refer to a parliamentary report of 1847 which accused them of being immoral and stupid and blamed these failings on the teaching of Welsh in schools. This slight was never forgotten and over the years it generated a toxic mix of inferiority and resentment among Welsh speakers. 'When I was growing up,' says Bethan, 'I remember my father saying, "If you marry an Englishman, I'll skin you alive." It's a natural thing for a minority.' But she hastens to add – with a twinkle, admittedly – that now 'Some of my best friends are English.'

It's almost time to point the Zodiac at Snowdon, but before we do let's slip through the mighty portals of Caernarfon Castle (speaking English is no longer a prerequisite) for a quick look at the Upper Ward area, the grassy higher level enclosed by the walls at the eastern end. The large disc of slate that rises from the manicured lawn is a symbol of the contradictions and ironies that make this Welsh heartland such a compelling place. It is the dais, or stage, upon which Prince Charles was invested as the Prince of Wales on 1 July 1969. Fittingly, the slate for the dais was extracted and shaped at the Dinorwig Slate Quarry at Llanberis, seven miles east of Caernarfon, in the heart of Snowdonia. Amazing as it may seem now, the ceremony – in which the heir to the throne wore ermine and held a coronet and the Queen wore a slightly silly hat – was watched by many millions around the world. It took place against a background of protest by Welsh nationalists, who regarded it as a provocative reaffirmation of English sovereignty over Wales (the day before, two activists had killed themselves with their own bomb while trying to plant it on a railway line to disrupt the royal train). In the month following the Investiture, Dinorwig Quarry closed without warning, putting 350 men out of work and knocking the stuffing out of a town that had lived and breathed – and died – slate for nearly 200 years.

This journey through North Wales is about the little as

well as the big people, and how they shaped this mountainous land in their different ways. For much of history, in fact, this terrain has been regarded as all but unshapeable. Roads were either non-existent or all but impassable for much of the year. Our route, the A4086 between Caernarfon and the heart of Snowdonia, wasn't completed until 1831. The London–Holyhead highway (now the A5), which opened up North Wales to much of the rest of the country for the first time, was built in the 1820s. In an era when scenic corners of Britain such as the Lake District and the Wye Valley – which we'll come to – were being avidly explored by the early tourists, this was still seen as a wild and dangerous place.

Partly this was pure historic prejudice on the part of the English. In 1781 an Englishman called Henry Penruddocke Wyndham completed a six-week journey through Wales in which he didn't see a single tourist or traveller. This, he wrote in *A Tour Through Monmouthshire and Wales*, was due to an erroneous belief that 'the Welsh roads are impracticable, the inns intolerable, and the people insolent and brutish' – none of which was true, he said.

Nowadays the most serious hazard we will encounter on the Llanberis road going out of Caernarfon is turning tractors – there's a sign (bilingual, of course) warning of this very phenomenon – while before us, spread in all their widescreen glory below the Zodiac's no-nonsense sun visor, are the distant mountains of the Snowdon massif. *Araf* – 'Slow down' – admonish the white letters

painted on the road surface, as if our flashy Ford wer
anxious to achieve those rocky heights as fast as possibl
when in fact it's so very pleasant to trundle through thes
gentle lowlands.

At the village of Pont-rug, the road crosses the Afo
Seiont – the Seiont River, which flows into the Mena
Straits next to Caernarfon Castle – on an old stone bridg
with low walls on either side. There are signs in garden
advertising *Gwely a brecwast* (you can work it out
followed by a triangular road sign warning of sheep ahea
and another indicating bumps in the road. Back in th
innocent 50s, people used to say this meant 'Brigitt
Bardot ahead' and think themselves very daring an
witty.

We pass the next village, Llanrug, and now there ar
water meadows to the right, grazed by sheep and bisecte
by a stream. The lines on the road are continuous doubl
whites, prohibiting overtaking in either direction. W
hum along at a steady 40mph, past low stone walls an
whitewashed cottages with palm trees in the gardens
And presently Llyn Padarn – Lake Padarn – comes int
view on the left-hand side and there are the first, rathe
shocking views of the scarring wrought on the west fac
of Elidir Mountain by the quarrying of slate. The terrace:
known as galleries, that were hacked out of th
mountainside are each 60 feet high and reach up to 2,00
feet above sea level. They are gunmetal blue, turning t
an unearthly lavender colour in the rain and shiftin
constantly along that colour spectrum as swiftly as cloud

pass over the sun. The colour gradations of the slate are one of the glories of Snowdonia. Nine layers of slate run through Elidir Mountain, and the different colours they produce, from rocks as little as two yards apart, have names that sound even more beautiful in Welsh than in English: *Cerriggwyrrd* (sea green), *cochrhywiog* (barred red), *piwsgwyrddcrychiog* (purple-green wrinkled) and *helygen* (willow). The galleries, too, had names, often taken from battles and wars – Crimea, for example – or exotic, faraway places. Thus a quarryman might get to visit both Abyssinia and California in the same day. And all without leaving Llanberis.

These days this small town is famous for being the gateway to the summit of Snowdon – the easiest, though not the shortest, walking route starts from here, as does the Snowdon Mountain Railway – and for its thriving outdoor centre, where you can climb up mountains and scramble down gorges. But until 1969 it was also known for being a community built on slate. The Dinorwig Quarry was established in 1787 when a businessman from Cheshire – and a great patron of cricket, as it happens – called Thomas Assheton Smith paid bailiffs to evict locals from the small-scale quarries they had been working on Elidir Mountain. This is the man of whom the locals say sardonically: 'You steal a sheep, you get hanged. You steal a mountain, you get a dukedom.'

A century later the Assheton Smith family was employing more than 3,000 men and exporting slate all over the world. In 1882 Germany bought 41,000 tons of slate from Welsh quarries and even Argentina managed 404 tons. The slate became roof tiles (water and ice have no effect on slate), billiard tables and laboratory tables, electrical switchboards (slate doesn't burn or conduct electricity), gentlemen's conveniences and gentlemen's tombstones. By the end of the nineteenth century the Assheton Smiths lived an opulent lifestyle on the profits, enjoying the run of a 34,000 acre estate on the Menai Straits that was stocked with deer, American bison, bears and monkeys. Though their wealth and lifestyle were grotesquely at odds with those of the quarrymen, many of the family were by all accounts fair to the men whose lives they practically owned. In 1887, for example, all the Dinorwig quarrymen escaped from Abyssinia for a day when they were sent to London to join in Queen Victoria's Jubilee celebrations.

But in the twentieth century, due to industrial disputes, increased competition and a drop in demand, slate was on the slide in Wales. By 1955 the quarry was still the main employer in Llanberis but production levels were a fraction of what they had been a century earlier. That year, Anthony Eden succeeded Winston Churchill as Prime Minister, the film star James Dean died in a head-on smash in his Porsche Spyder and 15-year-old Derek Jones started his five-year apprenticeship at Dinorwig Slate Quarry on a Monday morning, having left school the previous Friday. His first pay packet was £2. 8s. 4d. 'I used to give my mother two pounds of that for keep,' he says. Derek, a wiry, humorous and passionate man, is now a lay preacher in Llanberis. He recalls the camaraderie of the *caban*, or canteen – where the tea urn simmered, political campaigns were launched and choirs and football teams picked – and the hardship of the quarry, where 362 men died in rock falls between 1822 and 1969. Dangling from the mountainside on ropes, men drilled and blasted out the blocks of slate. 'It was dangerous work,' he says. 'You never knew if the rock face would go from under you.' And in open-sided sheds, men split these blocks into different thicknesses using a chisel and mallet, then passed them over to be dressed or trimmed to different sizes using a guillotine knife. 'You'd be dressing all day till your fingers were raw,' says Derek. 'Half past seven till five. Half an hour for dinner. Ten minutes morning and afternoon.'

Welsh was the only language spoken by the quarrymen, but theirs was a specialised Welsh, a language within a language, customised by local dialect and phrases that only the men understood. *Mwrw* (pronounced, roughly, 'murrow') described the tradition of counting slates in threes (so 12 meant 36); *dros Bont Bala* – literally, 'over Bala Bridge'– meant getting the sack. Strangely – no one is quite sure why – the only English words you ever heard spoken in the quarry, by the quarrymen at least, were those describing the different sizes of slate, for which there were no Welsh terms. Princesses were 24 x 14 inches, Duchesses 24 x 12, Wide Ladies 16 x 12 and Broad Ladies 16 x 10. The most popular size for a roof tile was the Countess, which was 20 x 12. Thus even the humblest of chaps can claim to have notched up a good few nights sleeping under a variety of countesses.

In 1960, after completing his apprenticeship, Derek Jones decided not to continue working in the Dinorwig Quarry. Instead he got a job with the council painting white lines and installing cat's eyes on roads. He believes that by taking this decision he has avoided a premature death, unlike so many of the quarrymen he knew. Looking at photographs of Dinorwig workmates from 1958, he says, 'Most of them are in the cemetery.' They died, for the most part, of lung conditions such as silicosis brought on by working with slate – though the quarry owners were always anxious to play down this connection.

In 1922 a doctor called J. Bradley Hughes, the Medical Officer of Penrhyn Quarry Hospital, responded to claims that working with slate was bad for you by writing: 'We have no case of Silicosis in this quarry of which I am aware, and I became convinced after four years' experience here that slate dust is not merely harmless, but beneficial.' It is not known whether Dr Hughes took up quarrying in his spare time in order to increase his life expectancy.

In August 1969, while quarrymen were taking their annual holiday, Dinorwig was closed and 350 men were put out of work, in a town where unemployment was already high. 'You might as well say it killed the community,' says Derek Jones. Slowly, the gaping hole left by the closure of the quarry has been filled. Dinorwig's old workshops now house the excellent Welsh Slate Museum, a perfectly preserved slice of history, and the quarry mountain has attracted walkers and climbers, while the lower workings are now part of a vast engineering project called a pumped storage system, which opened in 1984. This hydropower station – designed to produce electricity in an instant – is like the subterranean den of a James Bond villain. Deep below Elidir Mountain, where quarrymen once blasted out slate, are nine miles of underground tunnels and the biggest man-made cavern in Europe, containing six vast turbines. When the floodgates are opened on the reservoir high on the mountain, 2,000 feet above, these turbines are capable of producing a surge of power in a few seconds to meet peaks of demand. Job done, the direction of the turbines is reversed and they pump the water back up to the reservoir.

The power station is off to the left, across Lake Peris, as we pass the sign for Snowdonia National Park and begin the climb towards the Llanberis Pass. This pass – an east–west gash through the heart of Snowdonia – is formed by the Siamese lakes Padarn and Peris, and the Nant Peris River which rushes down the valley to feed them. The ruined castle, with its round tower, to the left as we continue to climb is Dolbadarn Castle, built in the thirteenth century by Llywelyn ap Iorwerth to control the pass. Beyond the village of Nant Peris, with its squat old church and combination of holiday homes and climbing hostels, the mountainsides of knuckly rock are veined with waterfalls, the white water creating a lacy effect as it falls around and across the boulders. The road narrows and steepens, 'while the scenery grows progressively wilder and the hillsides become barer and more thickly covered in rock fragments', reckons *Motoring Holidays in Britain*. 'On the sunniest days it is a wild scene; in cloudy or stormy weather a scene of utter desolation.'

So far we have been lucky. The rain, which threatens in the high swirling clouds, has held off. The sheep are sheltering but happily grazing on mossy banks above the drystone walls. There are dramatic fans of scree to the left, stunted, wind-blasted trees to the right and above them a forlorn-looking one-storey whitewashed cottage huddles high on the hillside. Then the wind suddenly rouses itself to buffet the Zodiac, the sky darkens and smoky rain clouds swirl across the wave-shaped peaks high to the right, which form the famous Snowdon 'horseshoe' of linked mountain ridges. Rain splatters the windscreen, the sun visor seems supremely redundant, and it feels as if we are driving up a funnel of rocks and boulders, as they muscle right up to the side of the road. These are the Cromlech Boulders, the biggest and weirdest of which looks like a petrified First World War tank, and behind them is a cliff face called Dinas Cromlech, where, in between factory shifts, a remarkable man called Eric Jones spent 'magic days' in 1962 learning to conquer both rock and fear.

Eric is one of Britain's great mountaineers. He made the first British – and fourth ever – solo ascent of the Eiger and is one of only two climbers to have conquered he Matterhorn solo. A slim, superfit man in his early seventies with a clipped moustache, he continues to climb, here in North Wales and in the Alps. 'To celebrate my seventieth birthday I climbed the Old Man of Hoy [the famous pillar of rock rising from the sea on Orkney],' he says matter-of-factly. If this were the beginning and end of Eric's story it would be impressive enough. But, not content with the extraordinary adrenaline rush of clambering on his tod and without a safety rope across the roofs of the world, he decided to combine his mountaineering prowess with his first love, skydiving, to take up the most terrifying and dangerous extreme sport in the world – base jumping.

'Base' is an acronym standing for Building, Antenna, Span (i.e. bridge) and Earth (e.g. a natural feature such as a cliff) – the four possible launching points from which a person with a parachute and a death wish can throw himself off. Eric has hurled himself from the top of the 400-foot high Fox TV building in Los Angeles, a 1,000-foot high television mast near his home in North Wales, and the Angel Falls in Venezuela, the world's highest waterfall at 3,212 feet. Limbering up between suicide missions, he became (with the filmmaker Leo Dickinson) the first person to fly in a hot air balloon over Everest (he has a certificate from Guinness World Records to prove it) and skydived from 10,000 feet on to the North Pole. Yet he is not a macho or vainglorious man. Softly spoken, he admits to feeling fear. 'The night before a climb, that's when I get nervous and start to think negatively,' he says.

'But once I start on a climb I'm pretty relaxed and focused.' He's had terrifying moments – on the Eiger especially, 'when I thought I couldn't do the moves' – but the rewards in terms of the sense of freedom and being 'totally in charge of your own destiny' drive him on.

In 1973 they drove him on for almost two months across the Patagonian icecap in the far south of South America with Leo Dickinson. For 52 days they battled Antarctic gales to pull sledges across a white wasteland of glaciers and volcanic peaks – and in the process they discovered a mountain that wasn't on the map. As a proud Welshman, Eric Jones called it Cerro Mimosa (Mimosa Mountain) in honour of some fellow Welshmen who had reached Patagonia before him, way back in the nineteenth century. And they started in Eric's home patch.

In 1856 a meeting had been held in the Engedi Chapel in Caernarfon – a plaque outside the chapel commemorates the occasion – to discuss the idea of establishing a Welsh and Welsh-speaking, colony in South America, far removed from the cultural and linguistic influence of the English, where cricket had never been heard of. Nine years later, in May 1865, 153 Welsh emigrants left Liverpool for South America aboard a converted tea clipper called the *Mimosa*. They reached Argentina in July and established the first of numerous Welsh colonies in the province of Chubut. Today in Argentinian Patagonia there are about 20,000 descendants of those early waves of settlement. This spirit of testing the unknown – of stretching for hand- and footholds you're not quite sure you can make – is imbued in the rocks hereabouts, for Snowdonia is the spiritual home of Britain's mountain pioneers.

Leaving Eric clinging halfway up Dinas Cromlech – it's windy up there, and still raining, so he's forgiven for not waving – we gun the old engine and continue up Llanberis Pass, crossing Pont y Cromlech, the old stone bridge over the Nant Peris River, and climbing up a valley of rocks and scree that look like the aftermath of some almighty crockery-throwing argument. A similar thought evidently struck the author of *A Tour by Car Through England, Scotland and Wales* in the 1950s. 'Weird and forbidding it looks, as though giants of old times fought some of their great battles here, hurling huge rocks from the mountain tops in a very ecstasy of fury.'

The steering is sloppy as custard and we seem to tack and slide through the snaking bends of the pass proper to reach the high point of Pen-y-Pas, at more than 1,000 feet above sea level. There's a car park here, but it's ridiculously difficult to find a space because they are bagged early each morning by walkers heading for Snowdon's summit – three routes to Snowdon start from here. There's also a National Park Warden's office, a café and a youth hostel, which was formerly the Gorphwysfa Hotel. In the first half of the twentieth century this hotel was the base for a climbing club founded by the mountaineer and poet Geoffrey Winthrop Young in the years preceding the First World War. This attracted many famous names in the pantheon of rock climbers – among them George Mallory, who embodies the most romantic and enigmatic of all mountaineering tales.

In 1924 Mallory was last seen alive as he headed for the summit of Everest, through swirls of cloud, with his partner, Andrew Irvine. His preserved body was found on Everest in 1999, but it gave no clues as to whether he and Irvine had made it to the top. The man who made that final sighting of Mallory and Irvine staggering upwards into legend was a geologist called Noel Odell, and he is associated with another hotel on the Llanberis Pass, the Pen-y-Gwyrd. We shall arrive there very soon, as it's just down on the left, after the Zodiac's overworked gearbox has enjoyed a bit of a downhill trundle from the peak of Pen-y-Pas to a point where three roads meet on a windy plateau, like lost and lonely strangers grateful for company.

Where better for a stranger to put up than the rambling and rather ghostly-looking Pen-y-Gwyrd Hotel, covered in creeper as unkempt as Ben Gunn's beard? This was once a hovel and was the subject of one of the most amusing anecdotes in the annals of early nineteenth-century travelogues (and those early accounts of journeys round Britain weren't known for their gags, it must be said). In 1838 an Englishman called G. J. Bennett stayed at the small hotel by the lonely road junction, noting in *A Pedestrian Tour Through North Wales*, his account of his travels, that downstairs there was 'a small parlour, carpeted, with half a dozen hair-bottomed chairs and a mahogany table'; he then headed, via a 'ladder-like staircase', for his bed in the loft, which he had to share with the owners and their servants. 'Sleep soon overtook me,' he recorded, 'and I should have continued to sleep, I have no doubt, until breakfast time, had I not been awakened by a trifling accident... I was visited by a dream in which the ghost of a lobster popped his head out of a salad bowl, and demanded upon what authority I had presumed to make mince-meat of his body, when a loud crash roused me from my slumber, and I found myself with my knees doubled up to my chin upon the floor, the bedstead having broken and deposited me in this unenviable position.' The Pen-y-Gwryd is much expanded now and has proper bedrooms rather than communal loft space. It is also one of the most charming, unusual and eccentric hotels in Britain.

Hotel and car will get on famously, for the Pen-y-Gwryd is marooned in the 1950s – and has chosen to be so, one should hasten to add. Few rooms have ensuite facilities, the basins, baths and WCs have seen a great deal of service, there are no room keys, televisions or telephones, breakfast and dinner are at set times and are announced by a gong and your breakfast boiled egg arrives wearing a knitted woollen cosy in the form of a chicken.

We can pin the hotel's association with the 1950s down to a precise date: 29 May 1953. On this day, the New Zealander Edmund Hillary and the Nepalese sherpa Tenzing Norgay became the first climbers to reach the summit of the world's highest mountain, Everest. The team that enabled them to do it, led by John Hunt, had trained for the expedition in Snowdonia and based themselves at this hotel. Four days later news reached London of the successful ascent – and Princess Elizabeth was crowned Queen Elizabeth II in Westminster Abbey, ushering in a new Elizabethan age. When, later that summer, England regained the Ashes from Australia, Britain felt as if she stood on top of the world, and it is probably fair to say that she has never felt so tall nor good about herself since. And the Pen-y-Gwryd stands as a monument to that moment.

In one of the bars a display case contains items and memorabilia from the Everest expedition of 1953: a map, woollen hat and string vest belonging to Lord Hunt; a length of rope Tenzing and Hillary used to tie themselves together on the summit; crampons and goggles; the sherpas' salary book, marked with their thumbprints in red ink because, being illiterate, they were unable to sign for their wages; and, bizarrely, a shrunken head from Peru, donated by George Band, who went to South America after the expedition. Elsewhere there is a fingernail-sized nugget of Everest summit rock mounted in a wooden board. But the strangest legacy of the Everest connection is in the Everest Bar next door. Here, the Everest team have signed the ceiling (apparently the idea came from the autographed ceiling of a bar in Vienna). The son of the hotel's current owners, Rupert Pullee, deciphers the squiggles: 'E. P. Hillary, Tenzing there with the scrawly T,' explains Pullee. This started a trend, and their signatures were soon joined by other mountaineers' and sportsmen's: Chris Brasher, Roger Bannister, Chris Bonington – and Noel E. Odell, the last man to see George Mallory alive.

Neither did it stop there. Demonstrating the broad popularity of the hotel's unique charms, the ceiling is now covered with the autographs of an eclectic and eccentric assortment of characters who have stayed over the years. These include the philosopher and pacifist Bertrand Russell – born at the other end of Wales in the Wye Valley, another wild, steep place – the actor Anthony Hopkins, the singer Petula Clark, the pipe-smoking Python Graham Chapman, the architect Clough Williams-Ellis – who designed the Italianate village of Portmeirion on the north Welsh coast – and the Welsh writer and broadcaster Wynford Vaughan-Thomas. It's a lovely fantasy to imagine them all staying at the same time, and tripping over each other in the middle of the night on intrepid solo expeditions to the non-ensuite lav.

The hotel is renowned for its old-fashioned, country-house-style gatherings of friends, and used to host annual reunions of the Everest expedition members (Hillary, Tenzing and Hunt are now all dead). 'I remember being in the garden and Tenzing picked me up and put me on his shoulders,' says Pullee, a keen mountaineer himself. 'I must have been light as a feather to a guy like that.' Edmund Hillary, says Pullee, 'was a huge presence – not only physically. He was a slightly shy man but once he got to know you – and he did know my father and mother and grandfather – he always had time for you.'

A century before the Everest team made the Pen-y-Gwryd into the most famous climbers' hotel in the world, the early pioneers of climbing were already using it as a base. In 1847 the hotel was transformed from the dump it had been at the time of G. J. Bennett's ill-fated visit when it was bought by one Henry Owen who encouraged walkers and climbers to stay there. In 1884 a thoughtful visitor presented Owen with a large leather ledger with a brass lock. He had had it embossed with the following title: 'Contributions on mountain rambles, botany, geology, and other subjects of interest connected with Pen-y-Gwyrd, with reminiscences, poetical and otherwise.' And he suggested that Owen should encourage his visitors to record their experiences in it. The result is unique and fascinating – nothing less than 'a running diary of the pioneer climbers of the nineteenth century,' says Rupert Pullee.

Much of it is practical information, shared at a time when reliable guides did not exist. 'We left the Pass of Llanberis at Blaen y Nant and ascended by rocks to the more easterly of the two tarns, thence bearing rather to the left . . .' wrote Charles M. Stewart of Newcastle-under-Lyme in 1887, thus helping future climbers to steer a successful course. Other entries are pure entertainment. On 5 August 1885 a versifying vicar, the Revd Hibbert Newton of St Michael's, Southwark, added these hilariously tin-eared verses in a bid to establish himself as the English William McGonagall, the Scotsman universally acclaimed as the worst poet in the English language. Newton was presumably inspired (not quite the *mot juste*, admittedly) by Snowdon's notoriously fickle weather:

Snowdonia! I sit down to write of thee
Personified into that sort of shrew
Such as in very life we sometimes see
Spiteful but giving promise at first view
To make one happy as a man could be.

A real writer – the author of *Westward Ho!* and *The Water-Babies*, Charles Kingsley – stayed frequently. He described the hotel as standing 'at the meeting of the three great valleys, the central heart of the mountains'. We are more than 900 feet above sea level here and, depending on your outlook, it is either a wild and free spot or, according to *A Tour by Car Through England, Scotland and Wales*, 'a dreary and desolate place'.

The Zodiac is a big, heavy beast, but the wind rocks her effortlessly as it blows down across heather and crag. Behind us is the A4086 and the valley of the Nant Peris River, which we have just driven up from Llanberis. If you take a left turn past the hotel we continue on the A4086, following the Nantygwryd River valley to Capel Curig. But turn the big, sloppy steering wheel to the right, and you push off into the downhill flow of the A498, and the heart of Snowdon's scenic glory.

The Snowdon massif is now on the right-hand side across the valley, a fastness of ridges and crags and the place where the pulse of ancient Wales beats strongest. The mountainous region known as Snowdonia in English is rendered as *Eryri* in Welsh – the place of eagles, though none are here now – while the Snowdon peak is called *Yr Wyddfa*, which means 'the Tomb'. In Celtic mythology Snowdon's summit is the grave of the giant Rhita Gawr, who made clothes from the beards of his slain enemies and was killed, so they say, by King Arthur for making his socks too small. Since 1820 there have been a variety of buildings on the summit and all of them, to varying degrees, have been a blight on the landscape. The most recent was a bunker-style café designed by Clough Williams-Ellis in the 1930s (hard to believe that the same man was responsible for the whimsical brilliance of Portmeirion), and described by Prince Charles, on a visit in 1984, as 'the highest slum in Wales'. It has just been pulled down to make way for a new visitor centre, built of granite and glass at a cost of more than £8 million and promising lots of curves and angles to blend with the surroundings. Hafod Eryri, to use its official name, was due to open in the spring of 2008 but fell behind schedule due to continuing adverse weather conditions.

This central ring of mountains, where kings, both mythic and real, once fought and hid among crags and caves and lakes, is now trampled over by hordes – 350,000 of them make it to the summit of Snowdon each year – wearing multicoloured, breathable fabrics and carrying GPS devices. Their ancestors did it in fustian and tweed and hobnailed boots, in the company of local guides. An early account of climbing Snowdon was written by the Welsh travel writer and naturalist Thomas Pennant, who undertook several tours of different parts of Britain in the eighteenth century, introducing Britons to their own land. When he climbed Snowdon there was no visitor centre at the top where he could buy a crayfish-and-rocket baguette, just a circular shelter of loose stones. 'A vast mist enveloped the whole circuit of the mountain,' he wrote in *A Journey to Snowdon* in 1781. 'The prospect down was horrible. It gave an idea of numbers of abysses, concealed by a thick smoke, furiously circulating about us. Very often a gust of wind formed an opening in the clouds which gave a fine and distinct vista of lake and valley. Sometimes they opened only in one place; at others, in many at once, exhibiting a most strange and perplexing sight of water, fields, rocks, or chasms, in 50 different places.'

The nascent climbing industry was the preserve of the leisured upper classes, and a boon to the impoverished local economy, providing business for hotels and guides. When G. J. Bennett stayed at the Goat Hotel in Beddgelert in 1838, he noted that 'Twenty post horses are kept at this inn for travellers, and eight or ten ponys [sic] for the accommodation of those visitors who wish to ascend Snowdon with ease and safety.' By the mid-nineteenth century, 10,000 people a year climbed Snowdon.

The narrow-gauge Snowdon railway – reaching nearly to the summit, with a steepest section of 1:5 – enabled

Victorian gents and ladies to reach the very roof of Wales without breaking sweat or indeed removing crinolines and boaters. It was built between 1894 and 1896 by a man with a familiar name, George William Duff Assheton Smith, who actually 'owned' Snowdon at this time (70 per cent of the national park is still privately owned). Its first locomotive was called Ladas, the initials of Laura Alice Duff Assheton Smith, the owner's daughter, and it crashed on the inaugural journey, killing one passenger. The railway was then closed for a year whilst safety modifications were made.

Like a lazy but intermittently ravenous monster, the mountain kills about ten people every year, usually in walking or climbing accidents, though it also casts malevolent spells in the sky. For these slopes are littered with the sites of air crashes. The worst was on the evening of 10 January 1952 when an Aer Lingus DC3, flying from Northolt to Dublin, lost control in severe turbulence over the summit of Snowdon and crashed in a peat bog near the shore of Lake Gwynant. All 23 passengers and crew were killed.

On a mild and wind-free day, Lake Gwynant doesn't look like a killer. A viewing point on the A498, about a mile below the Pen-y-Gwryd Hotel, has views of it south along the valley, a blinding silver looking-glass held in the palm of the valley. Just beyond this point the white lines disappear from the centre of the road – too narrow – a sign warns of bends for two miles, and it's necessary to concentrate on getting the Zodiac down in one piece, barely noticing the silvery waterfalls, clumps of purple heather and ancient drystone walling that pass in a blur. Eventually the white lines reappear in the middle of the road and we are cruising alongside the lake. From this position, the far bank of the lake and its reflection in the glassy waters are as perfectly symmetrical as a Rorschach inkblot test.

Leaving the lake behind and passing into the valley of Nantgwynant a sign warns that the road is liable to flooding. Here the public car park and the laybys are full. Car boots yawn open as walkers lace up walking boots and tug on all-weather gear. The footpath that starts from near the car park leads up to the Watkin Path, which climbs to the summit of Snowdon. On this path – built by a Victorian railway tycoon and politician, Edward Watkin, who naturally bestowed upon it his own name – stride the ghosts of two immense figures of British history. The first is the Liberal Prime Minister William Gladstone, who – let's set the scene – is 83 years old and has just been re-elected to his fourth and final term as premier. In 1892 his friend, Watkin, persuades Gladstone to perform the official opening ceremony of the path. In this Welsh heartland, on a rocky outcrop now known as the Gladstone Rock, the bewhiskered PM addresses a crowd of more than 2,000 Liberals, including David Lloyd George, on the theme of Justice for Wales. Seventy-six years will pass before the second figure appears. At this point the Watkin Path is doubling as the Khyber Pass and up it is strutting – all flaring nostrils and double entendres – the comic actor Kenneth Williams in the character of the Khasi of Kalabar. For it was here, in 1968, that location filming took place for *Carry On Up the Khyber*, starring Williams, Sid James as Sir Sidney Ruff-Diamond and Charles Hawtrey as Private Widdle of the Third Foot and Mouth Regiment. Comic genius. And pretty clever to save themselves a trip to the Himalayas or the Far East by using Snowdonia instead. A succession of filmmakers have done it, most famously in *The Inn of the Sixth Happiness* starring Ingrid Bergman and Curt Jurgens. Released in 1958, the film tells the true story of the English missionary Gladys Aylward in China during the Japanese invasion of 1937. Chinese villages were built in the area around Beddgelert and children from Liverpool's Chinese community were used as extras. Scenes were shot near the copper mine at the southern end of Lake Dinas, into which, on the left-hand side as we drive, a silver stream empties silently.

These hills are used to having stories grafted on to them. According to ancient Welsh chronicles, King Arthur was killed at Bwlch y Saethau, the Pass of Arrows, which is a ridge on the Watkin Path to the summit of Snowdon, and his knights sleep still in a cave on Y Lliwedd, one of the lesser peaks. One of the strangest stories of all – and one that goes to the heart of Welshness – is attached to Dinas Emrys, a solitary hill that rises like a balding skull to the right of the A498, just past Lake Dinas. You rather feel that Freud would have liked this one. On Dinas Emrys lived Vortigern, an early English king, who had retreated here to escape some Saxons he owed some groats to (or something like that) and was having problems with his house, which kept falling down. A local DIY wizard called Myrddin Emrys (the Merlin of Arthurian legend) suggested he look in his basement, and there he found, not a bad case of subsidence, but two dragons – one red, one white – fighting each other. The dragons escaped, the house no longer fell down and the red dragon was adopted as the flag and symbol of Wales.

Leaving the Sino-Japanese War and the pink blur of fighting dragons behind us, we set off on the final mile into Beddgelert, pausing at the T-junction by the Prince Llewelyn Hotel, which, on 21 September 1949, had the rare distinction of being struck by a meteorite (there's a model of this cosmic rock in the bar, the original being in the safekeeping of the British Museum).

Now the Zodiac faces her sternest test – crossing the ancient, extremely narrow stone bridge that turns at right angles across the River Colwyn. This double-span bridge is single carriageway, which is going to be tight anyway, but we have to get aboard first, and the 90-degree left turn is tricky. In some cases it is impossible. For the last few years, a succession of big trucks have been sent this way by non-Welsh-speaking satellite navigation systems. The result is bridge-lock, followed by much honking of reversing horns, and ignominious retreat back to Poland. Our problem is that without power steering, you need arms like Popeye to drag the wheel round, and the steering is so loose in any case that there is a perceptible delay between turning the wheel and the car responding. For a split second it seems to be crunch time for the offside headlight – but we make it onto the bridge, and, steering a nervous centre line, reach the other side unscathed. Let's leave the old Ford up by the Royal Goat Hotel and do some exploring.

Beddgelert, where two rivers meet, is one of the most popular tourist sites in Snowdonia, with an ancient, ivy-clad bridge, old stone cottages – in one of which Alfred Bestall wrote the *Rupert the Bear* stories – guesthouses, teashops and an ice-cream parlour. The mountain scenery surrounding it is dizzily spectacular and a short distance to the south is the Aberglaslyn Pass and Bridge, a gorge with a river and a bridge which was a favourite subject of Victorian stereoscopic postcards (twin images viewed through a device that gave a 3-D effect). To the north-west another exhilarating mountain road, the A4085, will presently return us to Caernarfon via the foot of the west flank of Mount Snowdon and the shores of Llyn Cwellyn. But for now we're going to linger in Beddgelert.

As George Borrow noted in his nineteenth-century travel classic, *Wild Wales*, 'the valley of Gelert is a wondrous valley – rivalling for grandeur and beauty any vale either in the Alps or Pyrenees'. This is all true. But people don't come to Beddgelert just for scenery. Whether they know it or not, they are inveigled here by a piece of eighteenth-century trickery that was way ahead of its time. We are entering a grand illusion, an ingenious arketing trick, and it started right here in this mposing, three-storey cream hotel 200 years ago.

'Beddgelert' means 'the grave of Gelert', and it refers to he ancient legend of the faithful hound Gelert, who was lain in error by his master, Prince Llywelyn ap Iorwerth, n the twelfth century. Llywelyn, who lived in a palace ere (or possibly a tent – it depends which version you ead), had left Gelert to guard his infant son while he opped out. When he returned he found Gelert looking heepish, with his chops lathered in blood, and no sign of is baby son. Assuming that Gelert had killed the baby, lywelyn stabbed the dog with his sword. Then, as Gelert ay dying, Llywelyn found the bloodied body of a wolf and eard the cry of his son, who was unscathed and had been iding under the bed. Llywelyn realised he had jumped to he wrong conclusion – that Gelert, far from having killed is son, had protected him by fighting a wolf to the death. e rushed to embrace Gelert, who licked his hand – and ied. Llywelyn laid Gelert in a grave in a field outside the illage and never smiled again.

Curiously, Thomas Pennant, who was very hot on egends, makes no mention of this tragic tale on his visit) 'BeddKelert' in the late eighteenth century – though he oes mention a 'famous mountain bard' associated with he village who wrote a poem about a fox which killed his avourite peacock. But by 1838, when G. J. Bennett and is overactive imagination stayed at the Goat Hotel, the ale was well established. Bennett even met a 'peasant' on he bridge we have just crossed with some difficulty who

pushed his luck by spinning him yet another sentiment
dog story in the hope of financial remuneration.

What had happened in the meantime? An owner of th
Goat Hotel, David Prichard, had made the story up. It i
possible that the storyline was suggested by existin
material, such as the poem mentioned by Pennant, bu
the motive was clear. Prichard did it in order to whip u
custom among the mainly English and middle-clas
tourists of the time. The cherry on the top of this finel
honed tearjerker of a tale was the grave itself, which h
shamelessly built in a field. And it worked. When Georg
Borrow stayed in 1854, in the course of writing *Wil*
Wales, he didn't seem to mind that the story was probabl
hogwash. 'Such is the legend,' he wrote, 'which, whethe
true or fictitious, is singularly beautiful and affecting.'

The grave is still there, and tourists solemnly follow th
signs on the south side of the bridge to the meadow wher
it lies beneath two trees. Some even think to bring flower
and lay them next to the headstone, which is inscribe
with the story. And as you read those words – 'The Princ
filled with remorse, is said never to have smiled again. H
buried Gelert here. The spot is called Beddgelert' -
remember to lift an ear to the encircling mountains. D
you hear the echoing laughter – *basso profundo*, naturall
– of a Welshman who put one over on the English?

Chapter 3

The North Cornish Coast

St Ives – B3306 to Zennor – Pendeen – Geevor Mine –
Botallack – St Just – A30 – Sennen – Land's End

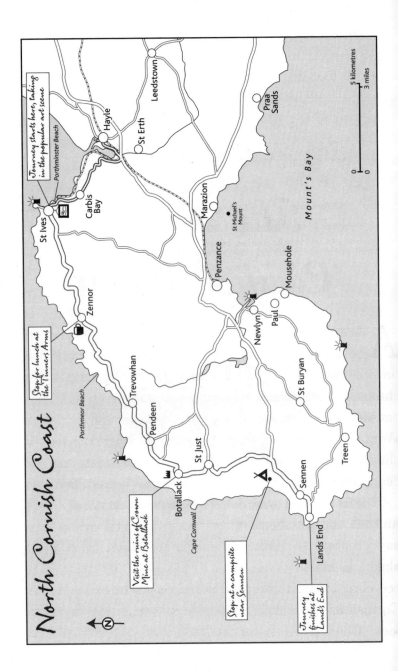

North Cornish Coast

N

Journey starts here, taking in the popular art scene

Porthminster Beach

St Ives

Carbis Bay

Hayle

St Erth

Leedstown

Praa Sands

Marazion

St Michael's Mount

Penzance

Mount's Bay

Newlyn

Paul

Mousehole

Stop for lunch at the Tinners Arms

Zennor

Trevowhan

Porthmeor Beach

Pendeen

St Just

St Buryan

Treen

Visit the ruins of Crown Mine at Botallack

Botallack

Cape Cornwall

Sennen

Stop at a campsite near Sennen

Lands End

Journey finishes at Lands End

0   5 kilometres
0   3 miles

The North Cornish Coast

A summer Saturday on the A30 in Cornwall: roof-racks and tail-backs, wailing sirens and a quick call on Bluetooth to tell your landlady you're running late. In the back seat a small boy raises his head from a games console on which he is playing 'Need for Speed: Most Wanted', and a chocolatey mouth is half-opened – until the question is killed by a parental lip-curl in the rearview mirror.

This is Changeover Saturday, when the guesthouses and bed and breakfasts of England's most westerly county say goodbye to their visitors for the week, stuff dirty sheets in laundry baskets and empty vodka bottles in to recycling bins, and prepare to welcome a fresh intake. As Cornish as shoe-leather pasties and ubiquitous car park fees, Changeover Saturday has survived the colossal

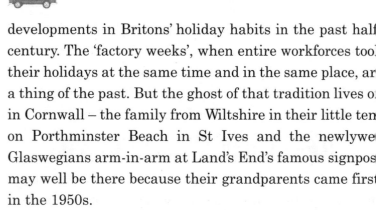

developments in Britons' holiday habits in the past half century. The 'factory weeks', when entire workforces too. their holidays at the same time and in the same place, ar a thing of the past. But the ghost of that tradition lives o. in Cornwall – the family from Wiltshire in their little ten on Porthminster Beach in St Ives and the newlywe Glaswegians arm-in-arm at Land's End's famous signpos may well be there because their grandparents came firs in the 1950s.

Following the austerity of the post-war years, and pr dating the era of cheap air travel, this was a decade c great expansion in domestic tourism. While factor holidays relied on the train, increased car ownership gav families freedom to explore glamorous new destination in their Sunbeam Rapiers and Austin A35s. And nowher in Britain felt more exotic and remote than England' jutting toe, with its – gasp! – palm trees, dramatic cliff and exotic-looking natives (some even said they wer leftovers from the Spanish Armada, which stopped off a the most southerly point of Cornwall in 1588).

The burgeoning holiday literature made Cornwa. sound like Ulan Bator. 'The inhabitants are, racially quite different from those in other parts of England reckoned the *Blue Book Guide*. While *Motoring Holiday in Britain* advised that 'It is in truth a very foreig land . . . the whole atmosphere of the county is differen from that of any other part of Britain.'

The natives may not have spoken Mongolian, but their was still a pretty isolated culture in the 1950s. One ma

ho can testify to this is Allen Buckley, an 'incomer'
om 'upcountry' (as the rest of Britain was, and still is,
nown) who made his home here. His journey westward
1 1957 was mercifully free of traffic jams and snarl-ups
he remembers more cattle, sheep and ponies than
1otor vehicles. But Allen was no mere tourist. Born in
3edfordshire, he had moved from Hampshire to take up a
1b as a tin miner, a job he would do for 35 years.
1comers were such a rarity then that he quickly became
nown as the Englishman. 'It seems odd,' he recalls, 'but
eople would say, "Do you know so and so? He lives in
Jewcastle." '

Allen started work in West Penwith, the bit that runs
om St Ives, where this journey starts, to Land's End,
Jornwall's westernmost tip and where this journey ends.
t was filthy and dangerous work, but, as he bent his back
3 granite workfaces many hundreds of feet below ground,
irectly above him the popularity of leisure motoring was
athering pace in one of the most scenic and thrillingly
vild parts of England. The road from St Ives to Land's
Ind – now designated the B3306, turning on to the A30
eyond St Just – was extolled in the guidebooks and
1otoring handbooks of the day as one of the classic drives
f Britain: '. . . as dramatic as any in Cornwall,' said the
3lue Book Guide; 'one of the most attractive of Cornish
vays,' asserted a publication called *Picturesque Touring
Areas in the British Isles*. And – in the midst of so much
hange, in both society in general and Cornwall in
articular – these descriptions hold good today.

The road crosses ancient and mysterious moorland
skirts the sea, twists through medieval farmsteads, and
keeps right on to the end of the earth, Land's End itself
Britain's very own *ultima thule*. It also passes above
mineral lodes that are rich in tin, and for which
thousands of men once risked their lives every day. The
twin faces of Cornwall – both dramatically scenic and
profoundly industrial – are perfectly encapsulated in this
19-mile stretch of road.

Before boarding our vehicle of choice for this chapter –
the split-screen VW Type 2, variously known as the
Kombi, Combi, Campervan or Splitty – on that road, let's
pause down on the harbour wall overlooking the beach
(one of four beaches in St Ives). Here, kids are provoking
herring gull wars on the wet, tide-sculpted sand by
tossing down scraps of pasty and sausage roll and a
passing woman says to her husband in Lancashire
vowels, 'They must have terrible heart disease, those
gulls.' From this vantage point, if you look back at the
town through squinting eyes – and the sun frequently
demands it – you can be forgiven for thinking that little
can have changed here in more than a century, let alone
50 years.

St Ives is an ancient fishing port tucked in a protective
bay on the north Cornish coast that now makes its living
principally from tourism. In front of you, clustered around
the parish church and the harbour, is the old part of town
known as Downalong – a tumble of old fishermen's
cottages, cobbled cut-throughs and higgledy-piggledy

reets with evocative names: Teetotal Street, Virgin
treet, Salubrious Terrace. 'Many of the streets are so
arrow as to be impassable for vehicles, and the tourist,
s he wends his way through their tortuous lengths,
ight fancy he has been deposited in some Italian town
n the shores of the Mediterranean,' says the late-
ictorian *Seaside Watering Places*, which has the
onderful subtitle: *A Description of Holiday Resorts on
e Coasts of England and Wales Including the Gayest
nd the Quietest Places*. This description of St Ives in the
ear that the Eiffel Tower opened in Paris could be about
e town today, with one glaring exception – the little
reets are still charming and parking is certainly a
ightmare, but the proliferation of pasty stalls and fish-
nd-chip shops is hardly reminiscent of *la dolce vita* on
e Amalfi coast.

Scan the heights that rise behind the old cottages and
t-throughs of Downalong and you come to Upalong, the
ewer part of town built on the hill which slopes down to
e sea. Here are the holiday villas and guesthouses,
hich began to sprout after the railway came to St Ives in
877 and which still put tourists up.

Superficially, then – certainly visually – St Ives has
anged little compared to most towns in Britain. But the
ifting and dynamic relationship between Downalong
nd Upalong, those two distinct parts of town, tells a
ifferent story. Martin Val Baker – a writer and gallery
wner whose father, Denys Val Baker, wrote scores of
ovels and history books about Cornwall – grew up in St

Ives in the 1950s. 'We would have fights between the Upalong and the Downalong,' he says. 'The Downalong were the fishermen, the Upalong were the farmers and miners, but also the incomers. But now it's the other way round. The Downalong are the incomers.'

The explanation for this change is to be found by sniffing the air – ah, that heady mix of recycled chip fat and joss sticks. For it is no longer the case, as *Black's Guide to Cornwall* put it in 1886, that 'everywhere an impression of fish pervades the atmosphere' as it did throughout the eighteenth and nineteenth centuries. This used to be Pilchard Central. Once, a chap called the 'huer' stood lookout on the cliffs, scanning the waves for dark stains on the sea that would indicate passing shoals of the little blighters, and scrambled the boats below by shouting 'Hevva!', which was presumably Cornish for 'Pilchards in extremely large quantities ahoy!'

On a walking tour of Cornwall in 1850, the young Wilkie Collins – one of the great Victorian novelists, who would go on to write *The Moonstone* and *The Woman in White* – came across a huer 'standing on the extreme edge of a precipice, just over the sea, gesticulating in a very remarkable manner, with a bush in his hand; waving it to the right and the left, brandishing it over his head sweeping it past his feet – in short, apparently acting the part of a maniac of the most dangerous character.' In fact, with this eccentric form of semaphore, he was issuing instructions to a boat in the sea below. The system evidently worked for, unlikely as it may seem, according to *Black's Guide*, 245 *million* pilchards were netted in one haul in St Ives Bay in October 1767. That's a lot of fish.

The passing of fishing on this industrial scale is elegised in the St Ives Museum – housed in the old seamen's mission by the harbour in which a video loop of flickering black-and-white footage from the late 1930s shows bewhiskered fishermen mending the nets, pilchard boats bobbing in the bay, and the morning catch glittering like semi-precious stones in the sunlight of long ago, all set to a romantic harp-and-piano soundtrack.

Pilchard numbers had already reduced dramatically by the interwar years and fishing in St Ives has declined ever since. Now there are just a handful of mackerel boats and lobster potters, the fishing families have moved to comfortable bungalows with easy parking in Upalong, and their briny old quarter has received the hanging basket treatment. From its quaint granite cottages, incomers flog fudge and pasties, crystals and Buddhas, and twee paintings of the Cornish seaside that would have the esteemed 'local' artist Barbara Hepworth spinning in her celestial sculpture park.

Hepworth was one incomer – from Yorkshire – whom St Ives has been proud to call its own. One of the finest sculptors of the twentieth century, she spearheaded, and is synonymous with, a colony of artists whose quality and ethos developed into an internationally significant movement – one that carried the name of St Ives throughout the world.

This area of Cornwall had been associated with painters since the prolific and peripatetic J. M. W. Turner visited in 1811, producing a watercolour of Land's End, which was turned into an engraving by George and William Cook for their topographical partwork, *Picturesque Views on the Southern Coast of England*, first published in 1814. Turner was followed by, among many others, the English Impressionist Walter Sickert and his mentor, James McNeill Whistler. They didn't hang around here – Sickert, deciding he preferred urban living to open seas, founded the Camden Town group of artists in London – but they helped establish St Ives as an artistic centre and by 1939 *The Penguin Guide to Cornwall* was noting that 'there has for long been an artists' colony at St Ives'. Six years later, by the end of the Second World War, that colony was turning into one of the most important movements in Western art.

It started with Barbara Hepworth and her second husband, the painter Ben Nicholson, who took inspiration from the sea, cliffs and moorland of west Cornwall – precisely the ambit of this drive. 'I gradually discovered the remarkable pagan landscape which lies between St Ives, Penzance and Land's End,' wrote Hepworth, 'a landscape which still has a very deep effect on me, developing all my ideas about the relationship of the human figure in the landscape.'

She moved into her studio and home in St Ives, called Trewyn, in 1949 and died there, after a fire, in 1975. Now open to the public, it is a small house with a garden and workshop enclosed by a high wall, which lends an air of secrecy and strangeness. 'Finding Trewyn Studio was a sort of magic,' she wrote. 'For ten years I had passed by with my shopping bags not knowing what lay behind the twenty-foot wall.' The answer is a garden as perfect as the trademark holes in Hepworth's sculptures, with a balmy mix of country garden flowers and semi-tropical vegetation – among which, over the years, Hepworth installed her works. The whitewashed workshop has been left as it was when she died; hammers and chisels lie around half-worked blocks of stone and dusty smocks hang on pegs.

She felt perfectly at home in her adoptive town by the sea. 'St Ives has absolutely enraptured me, not merely for its beauty, but the naturalness of life . . . The sense of community is, I think, a very important factor in an artist's life.' That sense of community and like-minded endeavour attracted world-class English abstract artists such as Patrick Heron – also from Yorkshire – Terry Frost and Peter Lanyon (actually born in St Ives), who used the plentiful fishermen's sheds as studio space (you can see these as you drive out of town). Their work interested Abstract Expressionists in the US such as Mark Rothko, Willem de Kooning and Franz Kline, and so it was that the brightest luminaries of the Manhattan art scene came – if not on bended knee, then with uncharacteristic humility – to a clapped-out pilchard port and bucket-and-spade resort 3,000 miles away from the buzzing and world-renowned hub of artistic endeavour Stateside.

'For a short time, St Ives was as big as New York,'

remembers Anthony Frost. Anthony is the son of Terry Frost and is himself a successful St Ives painter. His comment may contain a degree of optimism but the point is made. St Ives in the 1950s and 1960s was punching well above its weight in the art world.

A rare survivor from that time is Bob Crossley, who first came to St Ives from Rochdale, Lancashire, in 1959, the year that Mark Rothko visited. Now 95 years old, slim, bearded and sprightly, Bob lives above his family shop near the harbour and still paints regularly in both oils and acrylic. 'Painting's part of my life, like washing the pots,' he explains. Bob has always been an outsider, even within that post-war Bohemian enclave of artists. He left school at 14 and did piece work in a factory before becoming an apprentice coach painter and sign writer, and did not attend any of the fancy London art schools.

Refreshingly, his memories of St Ives in the 1950s are entirely unsentimental. While 'Terry Frost was very encouraging, a real friend,' Patrick Heron he remembers as being 'a bit conceited, a bit arrogant, and he didn't welcome me very much at the beginning. But he was very friendly in later life. He'd marvel at my fitness. "Do you still go skiing?" he'd say.' (The answer was always yes: Bob only gave up skiing at the age of 91.) His view of Barbara Hepworth is succinct: she was 'cool' (meaning standoffish rather than hip).

Although no artists of the stature of Rothko or Barbara Hepworth visit or work here these days, art is still a big thing. Of the 60,000 population of West Penwith, it is

six classic cars I'll be driving are revealed for the first time I begin to realise just what I'm letting myself in for.

970s Vauxhall Chevette – the last car I'd drive with a gear stick clutch pedal!

For one awful mom
I thought that the
producers might m
me swap my Morri
Traveller for one of
Scarborough's famo
donkeys.

Outside the Harbour Bar
in Scarborough, a Formica
heaven of pineapple and
knickerbocker glories, from
an age when waistlines
never seemed to expand.

The A169 to Whitby, across the N
Yorks Moors. Some of the gradients
exhilarating, but watch out for hidden c

Whitby – a haven for Goths!

The crew look down on an old engine house. The mine shafts stretch a mile or more beneath the sea.

riving the rugged Llanberis Pass – n east–west gash hrough the heart of Snowdonia.

Reading a map printed over fifty years ago, with my Ford Zodiac – which was pure rockabilly in its day – parked up and looking over the classical mountainscape of Snowdonia.

ith the legendary human ly Eric Jones, who, in his eventies, is still climbing rock faces and throwing himself off tall buildings.

The North Cornish Coast

St Ives, on the north Cornish coast. The VW 'Splitty' captures the town's spirit of Bohemian freedom.

Derelict tin mines – known as 'Cornish castles' – dot the coastline towards Land's End.

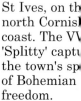

The crew capture the magnificence of a ruined Cornish tin mine. The mines are an inseparable part of the landscape and the people.

Feeling rather pleased with myself, having successfully steered the camper van to England's most westerly point – the spectacular Land's End.

estimated that ten per cent are working in the visual arts, which makes it one of Cornwall's major industries, along with china clay and tourism. Aside from Tate St Ives, an outpost of Britain's principal modern art gallery, and Barbara Hepworth's former home and studio, which attract hundreds of thousands of visitors every year, there are scores of galleries – and hundreds of artists working to fill them.

'There is still a fantastic, vibrant arts scene,' says Anthony Frost. 'But I suppose the difference now is that we also have the "factory galleries".' He talks of the apocryphal studio where paintings move along a conveyor belt and someone paints just the sky, another person just the sea, and so on. And some of the so-called art now on display in St Ives certainly does look naff enough to have been produced in that way. Take the beach scenes. The families on St Ives' most popular beaches, Porthminster and Porthmeor, bring as many tents as they do windbreaks these days (locals refer to the beaches as Glastonbury-on-Sea). But the commercial artists who paint these scenes always ignore the tents, which bring an unwelcome whiff of Millets to their whimsical seaside evocations.

It is time to leave the twisting streets and commercial shoddiness of the harbour behind and strike out west, for the landscapes that inspired the real artists. It was probably a mistake to bring the split-screen VW down to the curving granite pier on these narrow and twisting roads, for the fact is that these old Type 2 'Splitties', as they are affectionately known, are terrible at cornering. On the tight bends it feels like trying to keep a biscuit tin on a Scalectrix track. Then again, no vehicle is more redolent of freedom, sea and surf than this iconic marque. The Type 2 went into production on 8 March 1950 – the same day that Rover Cars in England unveiled a revolutionary car, Jet1, with a gas turbine engine.

The respective fates of these vehicles mirror the fortunes of the German and British car industries since the Second World War. Rover's Jet1 may have gone like a rocket – literally – but its fuel consumption was so horrendous that it never went into production. Meanwhile, the cheap and humble VW Type 2 (Type 1 being the Beetle saloon car) was soon one of the most popular and versatile vehicles in the world. The rattle of its rear-mounted, air-cooled engine (a mere 1100cc initially) and the two-tone V design of the front, with its large chrome VW emblem, made it instantly recognisable, and it came in a seemingly infinite number of variants, from the basic delivery van to the Westfalia camping bus.

About five million Splitties were made between 1950 and 1967, when they were superseded by a single front-window version known as the Bay Window. By then, the Splitty had achieved legendary status, having been adopted as their wheels of choice by both surf dudes – plenty of space for boards and a ready-made crash pad – and hippies, who painted the bodywork in psychedelic swirls and replaced the VW emblem on the front with the CND logo.

So let's point its distinctive snout – minus counter-culture customisation – along the cobbled wharf, turn right by the Sloop Inn (a pub where artists and tourists happily collide) and into Back Road West. On your right are the backs of Porthmeor Studios, the old fishermen's sheds where Ben Nicholson, Patrick Heron and Terry Frost all painted and which are now in need of restoration. Slowing down for beach-bound families and ambling ice-cream lickers, we climb past the dazzling white rotunda of Tate St Ives, which opened in 1993, and into Upalong, a land of Victorian guesthouses. A right turn takes us on to the road we want, the B3306. It is called Higher Stennack at this point, and it passes the former studio and family home of yet another world-class artist, Bernard Leach, who tends to get forgotten in the headlong rush to Tate St Ives and its major-league paintings by Heron et al.

Leach, who opened the studio in 1920, was one of the greatest potters of the twentieth century. He died in 1979 and his studio has recently been given a new lease of life as a workshop, gallery and museum. While living and working in Japan, he was heavily influenced by Asian techniques and aesthetics and he is better known there than here. Those Japanese tourists on the roadside are visiting the studio of Leach *san*.

But that probably won't stop them taking photographs of the Splitty – and why not? She's quite a looker – as she cruises past, now scenting the open fields. In fact, as you leave St Ives behind you can barely see over the high

Cornish hedges, bar views to the left of a rocky moorland
that is notably free of trees. The hedgerow vegetation –
ferns, convolvulus, cow parsley, pink campion and that
suburban escapee, orange montbretia – is reflected in the
polished hubcaps. The bustle of the harbour suddenly
seems a long way away. Then you twist over the top of a
rise and descend a surprisingly steep hill – and the
complex and slightly intimidating glory of West Penwith's
landscape opens up at last.

This is a land of stones. Dr William Borlase, who was
born along this coast road at Pendeen, was an eighteenth-
century naturalist who made a study of his native
landscape. Here were 'Rocks of that grandeur, remarkable shape, and surprising position, as can leave no doubt
but that they must have been the Deities of people
addicted so much to the superstition of worshipping
rocks.' From 5,000-year-old chambered barrows, or quoits,
to standing stones, stones with holes, round barrows,
stone circles, ancient chapels, sacred wells and medieval
crosses, West Penwith is covered in mysterious
monuments. The most famous sacred site is probably
Men-an-tol, a giant granite Polo Mint standing south of
the B3306 (not visible from the road) between Zennor and
Morvah. In the ninteenth century tubercular children
were passed through the hole in the hope and belief they
would be cured. If you catch people doing it nowadays –
and you're quite likely to – they haven't dropped a contact
lens in the heather. They're most probably petitioning
help in having a baby.

Let's park the Combi – the car park of the Tinners Arms at the hamlet of Zennor, four miles out of St Ives, is a good spot. Zennor is a quintessential Cornish moorland village – sturdy granite houses and cottages, a sprawling dairy farm, a church with a square tower, a chapel turned hostel and café and a museum that used to be a water-mill. From this huddle of buildings, walk back to the B3306. By crossing to the south side of it and following the footpath you reach the top of Zennor Hill, where the naturally occurring tors – stacked like poker chips – are accompanied by a 'logan stone', a huge lozenge of granite so finely balanced on the back of another boulder that you can rock it back and forth by standing on it (try doing so while taking in the extraordinary views, south-east towards Mount's Bay and south-west to the sea beyond Land's End).

A short distance to the south-east, across the heather, stands one of West Penwith's most famous landmarks, Zennor Quoit. A quoit is a megalithic tomb consisting of a number of upright stones and a capstone across the top, so it resembles a mushroom. Zennor's capstone, weighing nearly ten tons, has collapsed, and the monument nearly suffered further indignities in 1861 when a local farmer, in a fit of DIY zeal, proposed to convert it into a cowshed. He had already installed some stone posts and done some drilling when he was bribed five shillings to change his mind by the then vicar of Zennor, the Reverend Borlase, a grandson of the famous naturalist Dr William.

Katherine Mansfield, the short story writer and

novelist, could have done with a touch of that farmer's indifference to the ancient stones of West Penwith. Throughout her time here, as a guest of her friend, the novelist and intense visionary D. H. Lawrence, she felt spooked by the landscape, finding in it a kind of existential malice. 'It is so full of huge stones and I feel I don't belong to anybody here,' she wrote. Then again her mood of foreboding could have had something to do with the company she was keeping. You can see the house they stayed in from where we still are, on top of Zennor Hill – those slate roofs nestling in the hillside half a mile to the north-east, on the other side of the B3306, belong to Higher Tregerthen Cottage, which Lawrence rented during the First World War. The story of his time here says something about the mysterious spirit – the intermingled joy and darkness – of Zennor.

When Lawrence and his German wife, Frieda – distantly related to Manfred von Richthofen, the First World War fighter ace known as the Red Baron – arrived in Zennor at the end of February 1916, they were in retreat from the world. Lawrence's novel *The Rainbow* had been banned for 'immorality' and he deeply disapproved of the First World War and the so-called Christian civilisation that had produced it. Among the ancient stones of West Cornwall, he hoped to find a more authentic and healthy community, rooted in a sense of place. 'Cornwall isn't England,' he wrote. 'It isn't really England, nor Christendom. It has another quality: of King Arthur's days, that flicker of Celtic consciousness before it was swamped under Norman and Teutonic waves.' He also had a plan to create a colony of like-minded people, which he called Rananim. You could say he was looking for a paradise on earth. And for a time he thought he had found it.

The Lawrences put up at the Tinners Arms while they explored the area, looking for a house or cottage to rent. 'It is a most beautiful place,' he wrote in a letter to Mansfield and her lover, the critic John Middleton Murry. 'A tiny granite village nestling under high, shaggy moor-hills, and a big sweep of lovely sea beyond.' One day, out walking in the fields, they came across Stanley Hocking, the 16-year-old son of the local farmer. 'Along came this extraordinary-looking couple and they stopped to talk to me,' Stanley recalled many years later. Lawrence, he said, had a red beard and wore an old slouch hat and a brown corduroy suit – 'Very outlandish, very unusual for those days.' Frieda was dressed in a 'Bavarian type costume' with bright red stockings that she wore every day and which were a subject of conversation wherever she went. The couple said they were looking for a little cottage 'where they could live in peace', and Stanley said he knew of just the place. He pointed a little way up the hill to Higher Tregerthen Cottage.

They rented the cottage – one room up, one room down – for £5 a year. Lawrence worked in the upstairs room, at a table under the window which faced the sea. Here, in April 1916, he started writing the opening scene of *Women in Love*, in which the two sisters, Gudrun and

Ursula, sit in a window bay discussing men and marriage, and over the following months went on to complete the novel in long hand. When he wasn't writing, he marvelled at the natural world around him – 'the gorse in flame', a sleeping adder – grew vegetables in the garden, laboured in the fields alongside the farm hands, taught Stanley Hocking French – 'You never know,' he had said to Stanley, 'there being a war on, you might have to go out there one day' – and spent evenings in the farm kitchen, often to escape from Frieda after they had had a row.

For a time Middleton Murry and Mansfield took the adjoining cottage. This was to have been the beginning of the experiment to create the special community, Rananim, but it went pear-shaped. Lawrence and Frieda fought frequently – once he chased her round the kitchen table yelling, 'I'll *kill* her, I'll *kill* her!' – Katherine Mansfield hated Cornwall, and Middleton Murry was alarmed by Lawrence's desire to form some sort of 'blood sacrament' between them. Lawrence never spelled out exactly what he meant, but Middleton Murry feared it was 'some sort of ceremony of black magic to be performed amid the great stones of the eerie Cornish moors'. After just two months, the tension became unbearable and Mansfield and Middleton Murry moved out. It was as if the spirit of this strange place was driving them all mad.

There was worse to come. The war, which they had travelled so far to escape, was about to catch up with them. In the summer of 1917 there was an increase in U-boat activity in the Bristol Channel and the seas off north

Cornwall. 'The German subs were so active,' remembered Stanley Hocking. 'They were sinking our merchant ships right off Tregerthen practically every day. I myself saw three ships sinking there at once, one day.' Coast watchers and patrol boats policed the area, making sure that no one was showing any lights that could be seen by enemy vessels. In this climate of fear, suspicions evidently grew about what Lawrence and Frieda were doing here. She was German, for God's sake! They had been heard singing German folk songs, and she even had a German newspaper delivered sometimes. Matters came to a head on 12 October 1917. 'The military and police suddenly descended on him, searched his cottage and gave him and Frieda just three days' notice to leave Cornwall,' said Stanley. 'He was very bitter at that.' The incomer from upcountry had been given the order of the Cornish boot.

Lawrence and Frieda had done nothing wrong. 'I cannot even conceive how I have incurred suspicion – have not the faintest notion,' he wrote. 'We are as innocent even of pacifist activities, let alone spying of any sort, as the rabbits in the field outside.' So why were they picked on? The story that Frieda was spotted signalling to German submarines with a pair of red knickers is probably a confusion arising from her liking for red stockings. One theory, raised in a BBC radio document-ary, is that they were denounced by the vicar of Zennor, David Rechab Vaughan, who had been scandalised by Lawrence's anti-religious opinions, which he had made no attempt to keep to himself. But Lawrence was no doubt correct when he said simply that, 'People write letters of accusation, because one has a beard and looks not quite the usual thing.'

The whole experience triggered feelings of deep bitterness as he came to realise the degree of suspicion and hatred that must have been directed towards him and Frieda during their time in Zennor. She remarked that 'When we were turned out of Cornwall something changed in Lawrence forever.' He got his own back, after a fashion, when he later incorporated the story of his expulsion from Cornwall into the novel he wrote in Australia, *Kangaroo*. So at least he got a plot line out of it.

Stories germinate and intermingle as effortlessly around Zennor as the orange montbretia in the hedgerows, overlaid and prettified by the Cornish love of a good yarn. The most famous is the myth of the Zennor Mermaid, whose figure is carved on the end of an ancient pew in the church. In one hand she holds a comb, in the other a quince – or possibly a mirror. She could also have done with an ear trumpet too, for if she'd been able to hear properly, she never would have ventured from her watery home to stand at the door of the church listening to the heavenly voice of one of the choir members. That voice belonged to a local fisherman, Matthew Trewella, and as he sang he looked up to see the mermaid standing in the doorway. He fell instantly in love and, though the mermaid tried to escape, he followed her beneath the waves and was never seen again.

Myths are often misogynistic but, depending on the version you read, this one seems to apportion blame for the cock-up between Matthew and the mermaid roughly equally. The date and origin of the mermaid carved on the pew in Zennor church are uncertain but the myth itself comes to us via Greek mythology and medieval mystery plays, which were performed throughout Cornwall. So this ancient carving represents a continuum of superstition and belief, from the pagan to the Christian, in a place where superstition has always been strong.

According to lots of people (admittedly you tend to meet them in pubs), witchcraft is still practised up on the moors of West Penwith. It was almost inevitable, then, that Aleister Crowley would have stuck his satanic oar in at some stage. Crowley – who wrote on the occult and mysticism, took drugs, invented quasi-religious sex rituals (requiring lots of input from himself) and all in all revelled in being an extremely bad boy indeed – stayed in Mousehole, on the south coast, in 1938 and is said to have visited Zennor. At a cottage on the moor called the Carn, he is reputed to have initiated a coven of witches, held drug-fuelled orgies, conducted black masses in the stone circles – inevitably involving naked dancing maidens – and generally behaved in a satisfyingly Crowleyish way. A local artist and writer called Ithell Colquhoun who met him at this time was unimpressed and perhaps a little disappointed. 'There was no dramatic aura of evil surrounding the man,' she wrote. 'If I had not known who he was I should have assessed him as a not too prosperous country squire, with a kink or two.' Nevertheless, a rumour from his visit in 1938 has persisted: that he was responsible – in a way unspecified by the conspiracy theorists – for the death of a woman called Katherine Arnold-Foster, the former lover of the First World War poet Rupert Brooke.

The Carn, now a ruin, is still there, choked in under growth, to the south-west of the logan stone on Zennor Hill. It was later the house and studio of a celebrated painter of the St Ives movement, Bryan Wynter, and his friend Mark Rothko danced there, among the magical stones, when he visited in 1959. The house where Katherine Arnold-Foster was living is that grand late-Victorian gentleman's residence of honey-coloured granite blocks and large sash windows, surrounded by exotic gardens, on the B3306 above Zennor village. This house with the unfortunate Hitlerian name of Eagle's Nest, was later owned by the artist Patrick Heron and it remains in his family. See? Stories fly like sparks from this granite place.

Local lore, such as the mermaid myth, would have been passed down orally in the Cornish language, until Cornish died out as a viable, living tongue in the eighteenth century. Cornish was a Celtic language, similar to Welsh and Breton (spoken in Brittany), that was 'pushed west' by the tongues of the Anglo-Saxon invaders of the fifth and sixth centuries. By the seventeenth century, it was confined to this western tip of Cornwall and the last monoglot speaker (that is to say, Cornish was her only

THE NORTH CORNISH COAST

language) is generally reckoned to have been Dolly Pentreath, who was more than 100 when she died in 1777.

Dolly, who lived in a hamlet called Paul, near Mousehole, has been a real gift for the purveyors of warm-hearted Cornish tales of the pixies-and-smugglers variety. She smoked a pipe, she was possibly a witch and definitely a battleaxe, she spat and cursed in Cornish when displeased, and her last words – rather conveniently – are said to have been '*Me nevidn cewsel Sawznek*': 'I don't want to speak Sassenach.' The monument to her in Paul churchyard was erected by a nephew of Napoleon, Louis Bonaparte, an expert on minority languages.

However, it's likely that the story of the extinction of Cornish has been rather concentrated and simplified into the quaint and amusing personage of Dolly Pentreath. In isolated pockets, others spoke the language after her, though how fluently and naturally is debatable, and one of those pockets was around Zennor. A memorial stone on the wall of the church, to the left of the porch, commemorates John Davey of Boswednack, the next hamlet along from Zennor. He died in 1891 and is reckoned to have been the last person alive with a knowledge of old Cornish. He had picked phrases up from his father and kept them fresh in his head by reciting them to his uncomprehending Sassenach cat.

It feels right that the last authentic words of Cornish should have been heard here. The Zennor area, between the sea cliffs and the moorland, has been inhabited since the Bronze Age, 3,500 years ago, when the large rocks were piled into walls and small, lozenge-shaped fields were created. Notice how, viewed from the moorland tors of Zennor Hill, those tiny fields seem to spread out like ripples on water. The fields and habitations are linked by an ancient path that runs more or less parallel to the B3306: the Church or Coffin Path, which runs half a mile inland, crossing the fields to link all the farms and hamlets from St Ives to Land's End. One notable feature is the stiles-cum-cattle grids by which the paths cross those stone walls. They are bars of granite built over a trough, sometimes laid on the flat, sometimes configured in a shallow bridge, and spaced so that cattle will catch their hooves should they try to cross.

The road that became the B3306 is a more recent addition to the transport network of this remote region but, by hugging the moorland margins, it avoids the wetland bogs that can make the footpaths difficult, even in summer. In 1937 the Automobile Association had a patrolman based in Zennor: one Norman Jackson, who wore jodhpur-like uniform trousers and had to make do with a pushbike, balancing his toolkit on the handlebars as he rode the rolling north coast road on emergency call-outs. And one imagines plenty of those, as it's a road that requires drivers to keep their wits, rising and falling, twisting and turning and narrowing at certain points to barely the width of an old Austin Seven. Which is bad news for the Splitty. So before we move on, let's have a pint of Dutch courage in the Tinners.

There. The road looks at least an inch wider now.

The next hamlet along – a mile-and-a-half or so – is Boswednack, the home of John Davey, followed by Porthmeor, Rosemerg and Trevowhan. At each cluster of granite cottages and barns, the road narrows and contorts into virtual right angles, as if passing through a farmyard – which is indeed what it is doing – and the old bus has to be coaxed through with warning blasts of the horn, like a ship in thick fog.

These ancient farms exude a timeless, unhurried air. At Porthmeor, one of the cottages has been turned over to chickens, which peck about near your hubcaps as you slow to take the turn. A border collie dozing on the verge lifts her head in time to read your number plate. In a field next to the road is a standing stone. There are wooden telegraph poles, red telephone boxes, George VI postboxes set in walls, and cast-iron water pumps. A handmade sign warns of ducks and ducklings crossing. In the corners of fields old bathtubs are put to use as drinking troughs. Driveways sprout miraculous balloons of pink and blue hydrangeas, while red-hot pokers jut above old garden walls.

These suburban interlopers into the moorland flora are man's attempt to tame the wildness, but they never look quite right. More in keeping is the 1950s Massey Ferguson tractor that rumbles past, driving us right into the hedge, which delivers a schoolmarmish smack to the wing mirror. They're not to be messed with, these traditional Cornish hedges – seen end-on, they are A-shaped, and built of stone infilled with earth in which the vegetation takes root. The cabless tractor, its red livery faded to pink, is driven by an old boy in a straw hat and followed patiently by a red Morgan roadster with a picnic hamper tied to the sloping boot and flying the black and white flag of 'Kernow', old Cornwall.

This is one of those fun roads that attracts both bikers and vintage car enthusiasts. On certain weekends in the summer it is clogged with crocodiles of puttering bone-shakers from this or that owners' club, driven by men in goggles and women in headscarves (but no make or marque looks more at home than the Type 2). Triangular roadsigns double up in warning: the one meaning 'Road narrows' above the wiggly line indicating bends ahead. And the dotted white line down the centre of the road runs out as the tarmac narrows to a single carriageway.

When not negotiating the tight bends, the eye is drawn instead to the sea and you start to feel as if the land is running out – which it is, of course. Time to pluck the aviator shades from the top pocket of your Hawaiian shirt. There is sea to your right, sea in front, sea in your rearview mirror. It is a silvery pewter colour and it is often difficult to see where the ocean ends and the pearly sky begins.

At Treen, between Boswednack and Rosemerg, the road turns 90 degrees in front of the blancmange-coloured Gurnard's Head Hotel, with its name painted in large letters on the roof tiles. The hotel bar was one of the hangouts of the St Ives painters in the 1950s, and behind the hotel is one of the striking features of the coast here, the granite promontory of Gurnard's Head. It is one of several knuckles of rock and turf, called heads or points (and in one case cape), which jut rather like piers into the sea all the way from St Ives to Land's End. Standing right on the ends of them, with the wind in your hair, gives you a perspective right along the coastline and, with the waves crashing below, a sense of being *of* the sea without actually being in it. The springiness of the headland turf – about as loose as the clutch on the Combi – feels as if the land is already half-turning to seawater beneath your feet.

Gurnard's Head, poking like a blunt hitchhiker's thumb into the sea, is astonishingly rich in human history, considering its apparent empty wildness. It is the site of an Iron Age cliff castle called Trereen Dinas and in the Wayside Museum at Zennor there are 5,000-year-old saddle querns and mullers – hollowed out slabs and mortar stones – for grinding seeds and corn, which were found on Gurnard's Head.

In Treen Cove, at the root of the promontory, there are the remains of an early Christian chapel, and the ruin of an engine house marks an eighteenth-century tin mine. An arched doorway now leads to the sheer drop of a mine shaft and a yellow sign says, 'DANGER OF DEATH. KEEP OFF'. At the point of the head there is a concrete platform, all that remains of a coastguard lookout.

Another eccentric literary type, the willowy Bloomsburyite Virginia Woolf, found an affinity here. The lighthouse that inspired her modernist masterpiece *To*

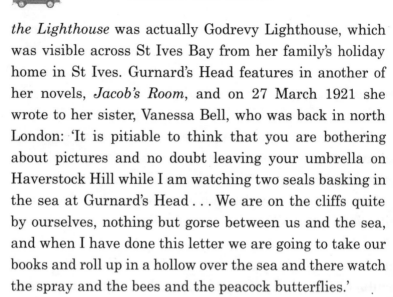

the Lighthouse was actually Godrevy Lighthouse, which was visible across St Ives Bay from her family's holiday home in St Ives. Gurnard's Head features in another of her novels, *Jacob's Room*, and on 27 March 1921 she wrote to her sister, Vanessa Bell, who was back in north London: 'It is pitiable to think that you are bothering about pictures and no doubt leaving your umbrella on Haverstock Hill while I am watching two seals basking in the sea at Gurnard's Head . . . We are on the cliffs quite by ourselves, nothing but gorse between us and the sea, and when I have done this letter we are going to take our books and roll up in a hollow over the sea and there watch the spray and the bees and the peacock butterflies.'

The path to Gurnard's Head from the hotel and village of Treen takes you through those prehistoric field systems and across granite sleepers arranged in gentle bridges between fields. Outside the farmhouse, a basket of courgettes sits on the tufty grass, together with an honesty jar: small are 15p, medium 20 and large 25, while a jumbo-sized one is individually labelled. It is 40p. In the slanting early-evening sun two lads of primary-school age are driving home a flock of friesians for milking – one on his bike, the other on foot, using a twig to give the rump of the hindmost cow an occasional tap (in truth the cows don't take much driving, they know the way well enough).

With a jumbo-sized courgette sitting companionably on the bench seat, let's continue west on the B3306 through the mining village of Pendeen, then south-west as the road follows the line of the coast, about a mile away at this point. The 1:25,000 scale Ordnance Survey map (*Land's End, Penzance and St Ives*) of the area we are driving is covered in features related to the tin-mining industry: 'Shafts', 'Mine (disused)', 'Tips (disused)', and so on.

Heavy industry – muck and danger, hardship and death – has haunted us all the way from St Ives. It's just that it hasn't yet really shown its scarry face. Now it does. There is no ignoring the many stone engine houses that dot the cliffs and moors of this westernmost tip. These boxy buildings with their tall brick chimneys once housed the steam engines that used to pump water from the mines. They are sometimes called Cornish castles, and in their bleak locations they do put one in mind of ruined castles in some sinister fable. 'They are just the tip of the iceberg because beneath them are literally hundreds of miles of tunnels and workings,' says Allen Buckley, the lad from upcountry who turned up here fresh-faced in 1957 to bag a job as a tin miner.

Allen Buckley worked down Geevor Mine, one of the mines served by the village of Pendeen, for 20 years, 'drilling, blasting, tramming [transporting ore on wagons], mucking . . . everything that needed doing really'. He also managed to fit in a history degree at Exeter University and to write scores of books on mining in Cornwall. He explains that the county is one of the very few places in the world where cassiterite, the ore that contains tin, is found and there is evidence that it was mined here as far back as 4,000 years ago. Tin was a must-have mineral because, when mixed with copper, it produced an alloy – bronze – that was ideal for weapons and tools.

In the centuries before Christ, a tin trade was established between Cornwall and the Mediterranean that has given rise to more tall stories about the connections and origins of the west Cornish. In the nineteenth century a story took hold that the Phoenicians came to Cornwall to buy tin and even that Joseph of Arimathea, the disciple who donated his own tomb to Jesus after the crucifixion, hitched a ride with them. In some even more far-fetched versions, he brings Jesus himself along – a possibility that inspired William Blake to write 'Jerusalem'. Though there is no basis in fact for this story, in the bookshop at Geevor Mine they sold postcards of Phoenician galleys right up to the 1980s.

At its height in the nineteenth century, tin mining in Cornwall employed some 40,000 people in 350 mines, from 80 feet deep to 2,500 feet. 'Along this coast at its peak there were two or three thousand people working in the mines here,' says Buckley. His fingers trace a series of lines on the OS map, starting on the cliffs below Geevor and moving out across the blue of the Atlantic. The mineral veins, or lodes, containing the tin stretch beneath the seabed, converging three-quarters of a mile out to sea.

Far beneath the waves, in realms usually confined to mermaids from Zennor, Buckley and his comrades tunnelled through granite to follow the lode. The gap they created in digging out the lode is called a stope –

chambers and chasms hundreds of feet high or long, often stained dark red with iron-ore, as if the rock is sweating blood. The overall effect is of a cross between a subterranean cathedral and a film set for an Indiana Jones movie. Every day thousands of men subjected themselves to this disturbing, alien environment.

When miners worked in the uppermost shafts of these undersea mines they could hear the rocks rolling and crashing about the seabed during storms, as the novelist Wilkie Collins described in his account of going down Botallack Mine, near Geevor, in 1850: 'After listening for a few moments, a distant, unearthly noise becomes faintly audible – a long, low, mysterious moaning, which never changes, which is *felt* on the ear as well as *heard* by it ... At last the miner speaks again, and tells us that what we hear is the sound of the surf, lashing the rocks a hundred and twenty feet above us, and of the waves that are breaking on the beach beyond.'

It turns out, however, that the sea was mild that day, that the unearthly sound Wilkie Collins heard was a mere whisper compared to when a storm is blowing: '... then the noise is terrific; the roaring heard down here in the mine is so inexpressibly fierce and awful, that the boldest men at work are afraid to continue their labour. All ascend to the surface, to breathe the upper air and stand on the firm earth; dreading, though no such catastrophe has ever happened yet, that the sea will break in on them if they remain in the caverns below.'

When Wilkie Collins visited Botallack they had not yet

installed 'man engines' – platforms that raised and lowered the men between the surface and the working shafts. Miners would be expected to use a series of wooden ladders, some as long as 1,500 feet. And after a filthy, dangerous and exhausting descent they would blast the rock using gunpowder inserted in fuses made from goose quill – a particularly tricky operation when you're using a candle to see what you're doing. 'Those who are not killed by accident perish of exhaustion and excessive toil,' wrote the French social commentator Alphonse Esquiros in *Cornwall and its Coasts*, published in 1865. 'The rock is hard and the ladders are so long. Very admirable is the stoical coldness with which they regard their fate. Cornwall is proud, and justly so, of her miners. Who can say what England owes to these men?' Nearly every day someone would suffer an injury – blow off a finger, fall asleep climbing the ladder to the surface after a hard day's work – and blind and maimed old men were a common sight in west Cornwall.

This was at the height of tin production in Cornwall, when, as Allen Buckley describes it, 'the main industry of the entire area was given over to mining: to take coal in for the engines and to take ore out. Then there was tallow for the candles, timber, iron. There was a foundry that just made shovels and picks. Everywhere there was industry. And money of course.' At the same time, Cornish miners were beginning to export their skills to other mining regions of the world. 'Cousin Jack' was the generic name for them. It was said that if you looked down a hole anywhere in the world you'd find a Cousin Jack digging at the bottom.

In the second half of the nineteenth century an estimated 170,000 Cornish miners emigrated – 20,000 to Australia, 100,000 to North and South America and 10,000 to South Africa with the rest scattered across many other countries. According to the *Cornish Post and Mining News* of 14 September 1899, 'There is scarcely a mine, be it in the auriferous plains of equatorial Africa, or the snow clad silver yielding reefs of North America, from the lead mines of Nevada, Colorado and Montana and the gold laden creeks of California, away down to the Southern States, to Mexico and the Argentine Republic, from Chile to faraway Tasmania, and back again to the diamond diggings of the Natal and the Transvaal where a Cornishman may not be found.'

As tin mining in Cornwall endured troubled times in the twentieth century – boom and bust, and bitter industrial disputes – Cornish 'tinners' continued to seek work abroad. 'For the Cornish, it's almost as if the world is their workplace and they go and mine there,' says Buckley. The industry finally collapsed as a viable concern in the 1980s, when the price of tin on world markets went through the floor. Now China and Indonesia supply 60 per cent of the world's tin, with the rest coming from elsewhere in the Far East and from South America, Australia and Nigeria. Geevor Mine died in April 1986 and the museum it became feels like a mausoleum.

The most poignant part of it is the 'Miners' Dry'. This block of offices, changing rooms and bathrooms was where the men – always and exclusively men: having a woman down a mine was considered bad luck – changed into work gear at the beginning of shifts, and showered and changed back again at the end of the working day. It was 'the heart and pulse of the mine . . . a miner's world, a gentleman's club, the only females being pictures of the latest Page 3 or *Playboy* pinup that adorned men's lockers, not a place for the faint-hearted'.

At Geevor it has been left exactly as it was on the day the mine closed for ever. Men's locker doors yawn open. Their overalls hang on pegs. There's still a sliver of soap in the showers. Allen Buckley remembers how filthy and discoloured they all would get from the clay and the mineral deposits. The small amount of iron in the ore would turn their faces and arms bright red. Standing in this silent place, it is not hard to imagine the banter and the fooling about – expressions of relief after nine hours spent toiling in a hole under the seabed.

After retiring as a miner, Buckley worked as a mining consultant and still lives in Cornwall, at Camborne, east of St Ives, where he has raised a thoroughly Cornish family and is accepted as an honorary Cornishman himself. When he came here in the 1950s it was, as the guidebooks said, 'a very foreign land' and an 'Englishman' was a novelty, treated with curiosity and, for the most part, courtesy. Now there are more English than Cornish in west Cornwall, working in the tourist industry and living retirement dreams, and, says Buckley, 'There is this antagonism towards the upcountry people.' Particular targets are the second-homers and buyers-up of guesthouses, who are inflating property prices to such an extent that locals cannot afford to live where they were born and bred. Buckley characterises these incomers as 'middle-class people who wander around as if they own the place, and put up restrictions, and treat the Cornish in a very patronising way, as if they had straw coming out of their ears'. And in St Just, the next stop on the B3306, one wag has scribbled on his dilapidated outhouse, in mockery of earnest visitors from upcountry, 'A traditional Cornish shed'.

St Just is the centre of mining in west Cornwall, a granite town, which grew up between the mid-eighteenth and mid-nineteenth centuries, and is dominated by a joyless-looking Wesleyan chapel the size of a bus depot. This is 'Deep Cornwall', where, in some pubs at least, conversations drop to chilly silence when tourists walk in. The town has a butcher who still has an abattoir on the premises – the easier to dispose of Englishmen who make jokes about the arable nature of Cornishmen's ears – and the circular village green, the Plain-an-Gwarry, is actually a medieval amphitheatre. Mystery plays were performed here – and are still re-enacted – but by the nineteenth century it was more popular as a venue for quaint local practices such as throwing sticks at chickens. Do not make jokes about this in the pub. Tin miners also took part in drilling competitions. The granite blocks on one side of the Plain-an-Gwarry are peppered with drill holes where tinners competed with hand-held hammer-drills to make as many 12-inch-deep holes as possible within a time limit. This is not amusing, either.

West of St Just is Cape Cornwall, the discerning person's preferred 'Land's End'. Cape Cornwall is one of only two capes in Britain, the other being Cape Wrath on mainland Scotland's north-west corner. A cape is a headland where an ocean splits, or – in another way of looking at it – two seas merge. In this case, it is where the Atlantic divides into the English Channel and St George's Channel.

Like Gurnard's Head, Cape Cornwall has lots of history – a Bronze Age burial site, an Iron Age cliff castle, the site of an early Christian chapel and a nineteenth-century tin and copper mine, which accounts for the chimney on its summit. But, crucially, it is not overrun with tons of people and cars, and all the mindless tat associated with the accident of being more westerly than anywhere else in the UK. This is because it isn't. The actual Land's End, some five miles south, beats it by a few hundred yards. But this wild and empty promontory *feels* the part. South-west off the cape are treacherous rocks called the Brisons (said to resemble General de Gaulle lying in his bath – head with prominent nose, big belly – and they do in a cartoonish way). On a coastline responsible for countless shipwrecks and much loss of life, the Brisons have been particularly bloodthirsty.

One of the most tragic cases happened in January 1851,

when a ship called the *New Commercial*, en route from Liverpool to Spain, struck the rocks in the middle of the night during a fierce storm. The crew of nine men and one woman, the captain's wife, managed to scramble on to a ledge on the biggest rock (De Gaulle's belly, as it were) where they were spotted from the shore at daybreak. But the storm was still raging and rescue was not possible. 'In this wretched condition they remained until about nine o'clock, when a tremendous wave rose and carried them off. Seven out of ten at once sank,' recorded a young Cornish writer called John Thomas Blight in a travelogue called *A Week at Land's End*. (Blight, incidentally, went mad, and ended up in Bodmin Asylum.)

The captain, called Sanderson, and his wife, Mary, were washed on to Little Brison (De Gaulle's head), while a crew member hung on to a piece of wreckage and was eventually rescued. All day Sanderson and his wife waited to be rescued, but the continuing high seas prevented boats from getting close enough. 'They were now to spend the night on the desolate rock, without food or shelter, exposed to all the fury of the wind and rain,' wrote Blight. The next morning, a Sunday, hundreds of people lined the cliffs and the promontory of Cape Cornwall to follow the fate of the unfortunate Captain and Mrs Sanderson. Eventually, a coastguard boat attempted a rescue by means of firing a line from a rocket – a device that had not been used before. The first attempt fell short, but the second reached them. Captain Sanderson tied the line to his wife 'who after much persuasion made the fearful leap. But when drawn to the boat, life was almost extinct and she died before she could be got on shore.' Captain Sanderson was rescued successfully and taken ashore at Sennen near Land's End.

Mary Sanderson is buried in the churchyard of Sennen parish church. The inscription on her gravestone reads: 'Sacred to the memory of Mary, the beloved wife of Capt. S. Sanderson and fourth daughter of the late Revd Thos. Wood of Newcastle-on-Tyne, who was shipwrecked on the Brisons and afterwards perished while being drawn through the waves.'

In 1853, as a direct consequence of the shipwreck of the *New Commercial*, the lifeboat station was established at Sennen.

Captain Sanderson took the quick – though not particularly desirable – route to Land's End that day. In order to get there now, we must return to St Just and continue south on the B3306, past Land's End Aerodrome. This grass airstrip has an air of bygone days, when pilots wore white silk scarves, props were of polished wood and had to be hand-turned, and biplanes bobbed along the grass like spin bowlers on their run-up. It still offers scenic flights, as it did when it opened in the late 1930s. 'Modern Holiday Makers', says an old hand-painted wooden sign they keep in the terminal building. 'See Cornwall with Scenic Flights Daily. Tickets 18/6. From St Just Airport to Land's End Car Park.' The flights were in a De Havilland Fox Moth that could take four passengers at a pinch, conditions that must have been distinctly chummy.

Just south of the aerodrome, the B3306 feeds into the A30, that workhorse of a road that has come all the way from west London, some 280 miles to the east. Beyond Sennen church, the last resting place of Mary Sanderson, is the First and Last Inn in England ('The last . . .' written on its northern gable end, 'The first . . .' on its southern), an old smuggling centre that has been a tourist stop-off for at least 200 years.

We are almost there. The end of the road, the end of the land. The Romans called it Bolerium and Arthurian legend locates it as the gateway to the lost world of Lyonesse, which now lies beneath the waves: 'the sort of place,' said Wilkie Collins, 'where the last man in England would be most likely to be found waiting for death, at the end of the world!' That'll be three quid for the parking, please.

The poor old Type 2 is corralled, like cattle at an auction, in a vast car park and, leaving the overworked clutch to cool down, you need to walk the final quarter-mile to the granite stacks, painted by Turner, that mark Land's End. On the way you run the gamut of a 'shopping village' and various exhibitions, including Doctor Who Up Close and Return of the Last Labyrinth ('An audio-visual show of myths, legends and history of Cornwall, with exciting special effects'). Land's End – 'The legendary destination' – is owned by a company called Heritage Great Britain plc, which boasts of owning a 'portfolio' of attractions that includes the Snowdon Mountain Railway and John o'Groats. They have created an impressive facsimile of a retail outlet on a ringroad, which at least succeeds in being a thumbprint of modern Britain – commercially rapacious and utterly charmless.

It would be unfair, however, to pretend that Land's End has been anything other than commercialised and disappointing since tourists started coming here 200 years ago. 'I thought to find a complete solitude,' wrote Walter White in *A Londoner's Walk to the Land's End*, published in 1861, 'but a public house, the Land's End Inn, and outbuildings stand near the cliff, and are felt to be an intrusion; and the more unnecessary, as "good entertainment" is to be got at Sennen, but half a mile off.' *The Penguin Guide to Cornwall* of 1939 warns that 'even the most expert photographers are hard put to it to exclude from their pictures the enormous hotel'.

To get anything out of Land's End today, that's exactly what you have to do: screen out the tat. The most annoying thing about Land's End is that the final, final bit of England is out of bounds, fenced off behind notices that warn, 'No unauthorised persons beyond this point'. It is not possible to get close enough to make out – and there is no information to help you – the various outcrops and stacks of granite that were given such romantic names in the eighteenth and nineteenth centuries – the Armed Knight, Dr Syntax's Head, Dr Johnson's Head.

But by standing with your back to England, it is possible to ignore it all for long enough to think solitary thoughts and marvel about how spectacular it nevertheless is. You may even feel a soft spot for that tubercular genius D. H. Lawrence, who in coming to west Cornwall turned his back on the sides of England he hated. 'It is so lovely to recognise the non-human elements: to hear the rain like a song, to feel the wind going by one,' he wrote.

And as you gaze across the top of the Longships Lighthouse, and strain to spot the ghostly wisps of the Scilly Isles on the western horizon, it's a good time to reflect that Cornwall remains a place apart from the rest of England. Yes, it has changed since the 1950s. An Englishman is no longer a novelty, and the pasties don't break your teeth, but up on the moors and down by the sea the old stones still hold an eternity of secrets. And you feel that, somehow. This exhilarating drive has merely liberated a tiny fraction of those secrets.

Chapter 4

The Lake District

Keswick – Castlerigg Stone Circle – A591 to Grasmere and Ambleside – unclassified road, 'The Struggle', to Kirkstone Pass – A592 to Penrith and M6

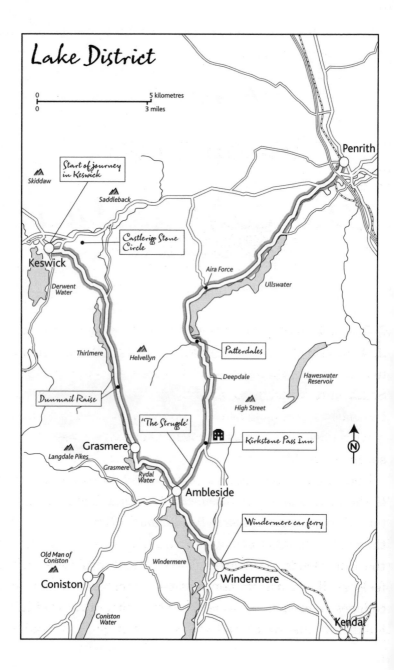

The Lake District

R AIN. IT DRUMS LIKE THOUGHTFUL fingers on the soft vinyl roof. This is the Lake District, after all, home to the wettest inhabited place in Britain – a hamlet called Seathwaite, which is, thankfully, not on our route. There, the native Cumbrians are born with webbed feet and don't realise they can take cagoules *off* till they're about seven years old.

The weather can change quickly though, that's the joy of the place – and the beauty of driving a Triumph soft-top, which, before long, will be folded away in order to feel the silage-scented air whistling up our nostrils. For now, the rain clouds swirl around the encircling fells and it feels as if we are in one of those panoramic Polaroid collages – clockwise from the south-east, the swelling bulks and peaks of Helvellyn, Castlerigg Fell, Walla

Crags, Cat Bells, Grisedale Pike, Skiddaw, Blencathra and the Dodds form a mighty rampart of many miles in circumference. And bang in the middle, like the hub of a wheel, is a much smaller circle – a mere 100 feet across. It consists of 38 monolithic stones (with a further ten forming an enclosure) standing on a low, flat-topped hill outside the town of Keswick.

This is Castlerigg Stone Circle and its setting and arrangement are uncannily affecting. The field is like a raised stage in a theatre-in-the-round. The shapes of the stones echo the peaks of the surrounding fells. The Bronze Age bods who dragged and erected these blocks of Borrowdale volcanic rock in this place, in precisely this configuration, four or five thousand years ago may have been wearing woolly-mammoth loincloths, but they had a highly developed sense of drama. This is one of the most atmospheric ancient sites in Britain. Standing in this windswept spot you feel you are at the perfectly still centre of a constantly changing world.

Somebody else had a similar idea about the Lakes. And from now on, he will be popping up with fair frequency because he is, quite simply, one of the most important figures in the development of travel and tourism in Britain. His name is William Wordsworth, the Romantic poet and spiritual father of his native Lake District. But he's hardly likely to hop in on the passenger side because his chosen means of transport was only ever his own legs. This doesn't mean he can't keep pace, however – even given the mean 1991cc engine that powers the Triumph

'R3A we're nipping along in today. Wordsworth's friend nd acolyte, the opium-eater and essayist Thomas De Quincey, calculated in *Recollections of the Lakes and the Lake Poets*, published between 1834 and 1840, that with is legs 'Wordsworth must have traversed a distance of 75 to 180,000 English miles.' Those legs, by the way, vere 'certainly not ornamental', and indeed Wordsworth imself 'was, upon the whole, not a well-made man' who valked like 'some sort of insect which advances by an blique motion'. There's quite a lot more in this vein. Vhat did Wordsworth *do* to De Quincey to deserve such a leeful trashing, one wonders?

Wordsworth walked virtually every inch of the route ve're taking – from Keswick, where his fellow poets Robert Southey and Samuel Taylor Coleridge lived, via he 'Druids' Circle' of Castlerigg, to the cottage at Grasmere where he sat versifying in a peculiar milking tool of a chair. It must have worked, as some of the most eautiful and revolutionary poems in the English anguage were written while his oddly-shaped body was olded into it.

After dashing off some lines about a high pass called Kirkstone, Wordsworth takes us there himself, up one of he most dramatic road passes in Britain; across the fells the Norse word *fell*, a legacy of the Vikings who colonised he Lakes in the eighth century, means hill or mountain) ve descend to a lake where he had one of the spookiest and most character-forming experiences of his childhood, and later in life found inspiration to write a poem that, after 200 years, remains as familiar as your mobile's ringtone. Actually, the one place he hasn't been around these parts, nor could ever have dreamt would come into existence, is our destination – the M6 at Penwith.

A bright red, two-seater 1960 Triumph TR3A will take us there. Manufactured between 1957 and 1962, the TR3A is an updated version of the TR3, the first production car to be fitted with disc brakes as standard. It is sporty and stylish, in a bug-eyed way, and handles the narrow bends and gradients of the Lakes with insouciance – even if you can't always see what may be coming up behind, due to the minuscule size of the rearview mirror. As with all thoroughbreds, however, she is skittish and requires delicate clutch control – otherwise she withdraws cooperation and sulks off in a humiliating series of bunny hops. One of her most charming features is her small, perfectly formed windscreen wipers, miracles of precision engineering that sweep and swish like dainty hands. And we are in the right place to test them out. Parked near the stone circle, in the midst of that glorious Lakeland panorama, the Triumph stands out like a bead of fresh blood on a faded tapestry.

But let's not leave quite yet, even if you are starting to feel the muddy rainwater seeping into your comfortable driving shoes and the allure of this wild place is fading a little, because Castlerigg is worth dwelling on. The early visitors to the Lakes, in the eighteenth century, would certainly have been more likely to feel the damp in their boots than the fire in their souls, for stone circles just weren't regarded as cool and touchy-feely spiritual as they are now. Perhaps in an age when religious faith was absorbed and held by practically everyone, sites that may possibly have been used for pagan worship were regarded with distaste – hence Castlerigg used to be called, erroneously, the Druidical or Druids' Circle. Nowadays, in a society of many faiths and none, when people dabble in all kinds of New Age beliefs, the power of old places like Castlerigg is felt or imagined afresh by all sorts of people, from students who skim frisbees across the grassy circle enclosed by the stones to cowled enthusiasts who bang drums and chant.

Nor were people taken with wild landscapes back in the eighteenth century. The romantic poet John Keats, who visited in 1818 during a walking holiday of the Lakes, would have been amazed by how venerated the site has become. He wove a description of Castlerigg and the surrounding fells into his unfinished epic poem *Hyperion*, calling it 'A dismal cirque/Of Druid stones, upon a forlorn moor'. He was, admittedly, fed up and coughing blood – the first sign of the tuberculosis that would kill him three years later – but his impression of the 'forlorn moor' was consistent with an age in which wild landscapes were regarded as ugly and dangerous. Wordsworth reckoned that before the time of the poet Thomas Gray – who wrote *Elegy Written in a Country Churchyard* and died in 1771 – 'there is not, I believe, a single English traveller whose published writings would disprove the assertion that, where precipitous rocks and mountains are mentioned at all, they are spoken of as objects of dislike and fear, and not of admiration'.

So think about this, because it goes to the heart of *Britain's Best Drives*: finding inspiration in Britain's beautiful and varied landscapes is not a natural thing like sleeping or enjoying chocolate. It has been learned. And, more than anyone, the person who taught us is Wordsworth.

It's stopped raining and sunlight is now patching the fellsides over to the west. Time to fold back the soft top and hit the road.

From the field containing the stone circle, we take the narrow lane to the west of it that runs dead straight to join the A591. The outskirts of Keswick are less than a mile to the right. Grasmere and Ambleside – and the geographical and spiritual heart of the Lakes – are respectively, about 12 and 16 miles to the left. It can be a fast and dicey road, this. Coming out of Keswick, a blue sign warns: '393 casualties in 5 years. Drive carefully.'

Dead ahead, the tree-covered Castlerigg Fell faces us down as we speed between drystone walling to the left and hedges to the right, with views ahead and below us of the green valley bottom. Whitewashed farmhouses huddle in the lee of high fellsides, as if permanently anticipating a storm, and a triangular sign warns of deer for six miles. On two occasions between here and Grasmere the north and south carriageways split around outcrops of rock, like a river flowing round a boulder. As the fells seem to rise around us like a guard of honour –

Helvellyn, at 3,119 feet the third highest peak in both the Lakes and in England, is to the left – there is a palpable sense of entering a realm quite different in appearance and feel from anywhere else in Britain.

Wordsworth likened the topography to a wheel, with a hub or 'nave' at its centre, and he located this hub on a cloud hanging midway between the summits of Sca Fell and Great Gable (he had apparently not been raiding De Quincey's opium cabinet when he came up with this). The spokes of the wheel are the valleys and lakes that emanate from this central point. Actually, on a map, those lakes and valleys look less like wheel spokes than like wriggling protozoic creatures. Whatever the simile, the Lakes are small – the National Park covers just 885 square miles and extends 33 miles east to west and 40 miles north to south – and neither its mountains nor its bodies of water stand any kind of size comparison with the great mountains and lakes of Europe. Yet the Lake District is one of the most beautiful corners of the continent, attracting 11 million visitors a year from all over the world.

A Victorian guidebook writer called M. J. B. Baddeley considered this apparent contradiction between the Lakeland's modest size and proportions and its popularity in *The Thorough Guide to the Lakes*, first published in 1880:

In the effect which it produces on the eye and mind of the spectator, mountain scenery is much more dependent on the proportion of its component parts than on the foot-and-line measurement of any one of them, and in this attribute of proportion there is probably no 'beauty-spot' in the world which can equal English Lakeland. It is not sufficient that a given area should contain elements of the beautiful; it must contain nothing else. Every stretch of dull moorland intervening between lake, valley and mountain-top . . . is so much loss. Not only is it an eyesore in itself, but it dwarfs the apparent height, and consequently the impressiveness, of the mountains beyond it, and not unfrequently keeps so far apart the picturesque elements of a landscape as to make them appear mere straggling outposts of different scenes. The English Lake District is, of course, not entirely free from these blemishes, but it contains them to a smaller degree than any other mountain-country. Its characteristic charm may be said to be the thoroughly accordant blending of mountain, valley, and lake, in a succession of pictures whose variety is only equalled by their unity.

Or, to put it another way, it hasn't got any grotty or boring bits. It's all filling and no bread. And we are heading straight for the richest part of that filling.

The lake that presently appears on the right-hand side, its far shore planted with conifers to the water's edge, has guilty secrets, along with jumbo pike, in its depths. The crenellated building on the right-hand side of the road isn't a haunted castle in a gothic novel but a 'straining well' – a water treatment works – and the lake isn't actually a lake. It is a reservoir that has provided water for the City of Manchester for more than a century. Before that, the valley was a community and the lake, edged with cliffs and bluffs, was hourglass-shaped and commonly referred to as two separate bodies of water, Leathes Water and Wythburn Water. Around it there were a few houses, a church, a couple of inns and the palatial Armboth House. 'Its singular beauty is its being almost intersected in the middle by two peninsulas, that are joined by a bridge in a taste suitable to the genius of the place, which serves for an easy communication among the shepherds that dwell on the opposite banks,' wrote Thomas West in one of the earliest guidebooks to the area, *A Guide to the Lakes, in Cumberland, Westmorland and Lancashire*, which was first published in 1778. Twenty years after this observation, Wordsworth and Coleridge were in the habit of leaving their respective houses in Grasmere and Keswick and using the valley as a meeting point.

By the 1870s the rapidly expanding conurbation of Manchester was in need of a source of fresh water for its inhabitants. The Thirlmere valley was chosen as the ideal site for a reservoir – the surrounding fells formed a natural bowl that would be easy to fill with water (just leave the plug in during April) and the high elevation made it easy to get the stuff out. Despite local opposition provided by the Thirlmere Defence Association (both local rustics and influential do-gooders), the project was eventually given the go-ahead and a dam was constructed at the northern end.

Between 1894 and 1918 the level of the lake was increased by nearly 60 feet, obliterating the pleasing hourglass shape and the cliffs that edged it, and displacing some 200 people. 'The old charm of its shores has quite vanished, and the sites of its legends are hopelessly altered, so that to walk along either side is a mere sorrow to anyone who cared for it before,' wrote the artist and author W. G. Collingwood in *The Lake Counties*, first published in 1902. Collingwood also had a go at that dratted recent phenomenon, the motor car: 'the formality of [Thirlmere's] roads, beloved of car drivers and cyclists, deforms the hillsides like a scar on a face.'

Once, Wythburn, on the eastern shore near the southern end, was a hamlet with a school, a scattering of houses, a church and, opposite the church, the Nag's Head Inn. The inn is recommended by Baddeley in *The Thorough Guide* as the best starting place for the ascent of Helvellyn ('Letter-box cleared abt. 4.45', he adds helpfully). Dorothy Wordsworth, William's sister, records in her journals that on 15 October 1800, 'I walked with [William] to Wytheburn [sic], and he went on to Keswick. I drank tea, and supped at Mr Simpson's [the Nag's Head]. A very cold frosty air and a spangled sky in returning . . . Wytheburn looked very wintry, but yet there was a foxglove blossoming by the roadside.'

The poets and their groupies used to rendezvous at a rock nearby, where, according to Dorothy's journals, on

4 May 1802 they carved their initials. This rock, known as the Rock of Names, was blown up to make way for the reservoir, but someone rescued the bits and glued them back together. The reconstituted rock, bearing the initials W. W. and S. T. C., is now in the garden of the Wordsworth Museum in Grasmere. The man who did this was no mere poetic anorak who would rootle in dustbins for his heroes' toast crusts. His name was Canon Hardwicke Rawnsley and he is another enlightened and impassioned figure of the nineteenth century to whom we owe the preservation of so much of our heritage.

Apart from the remains of walls and tree stumps that are sometimes visible when the water level drops, 'Wytheburn's modest house of prayer/ As lowly as the lowliest dwelling', as Wordsworth described the church in *The Waggoner*, is all that's left of this nexus of energy and creativity. Small and whitewashed, it is tucked off the A591 on the left-hand side as we drive south. The body of the church was built in 1740, the semi-circular chancel being added in 1872. It is a deathly quiet, forlorn-feeling space, as if in permanent mourning for the vanished piece of world it once served. The former community may have been tiny, but it still managed to serve up two young men – Privates Joe Sandham and Alfred Bell – for slaughter at the Battle of the Somme in 1916. They are commemorated on a wall plaque. Joe, who was 20, had lived at Helvellyn House, just across the road from the church. Alfred, who was born in Wythburn, had been working for Manchester Corporation on the construction of the reservoir before the war. There is scarcely a church in the whole of Britain, be it ever so small or remote, that doesn't commemorate at least one soldier killed in the First World War.

Rising, falling and twisting, the road clears the southern end of Thirlmere, then the carriageways divide briefly before we begin the gradual ascent of Dunmail Raise, the gentle pass that marks the old boundary between Cumberland and Westmorland and takes us into the Vale of Grasmere. In a layby on the pass is a post-war, sentry-style Automobile Association box in its original back and yellow livery, one of just 21 left out of the thousand or so once located at remote roadside spots. The box was originally used as a base and shelter for the local AA patrolman and later as a phone box for members who were issued with a special key. As well as a telephone, the box contained a fire extinguisher, maps, and probably a jar of mint imperials, a tobacco-filled pipe ready for lighting, and a copy of *The Lady* so you had plenty to do till the patrolman arrived.

What he arrived on would have depended on the era. The AA was formed in 1905 for a very modern-sounding sort of reason – to hinder the police in their attempts to persecute motorists for exceeding the then 20mph speed limit. Patrolmen, called 'scouts' back then, would recce popular routes on pushbikes, warning AA members – identifiable by a badge on their cars – of speed traps ahead. By 1912 there were 950 scouts operating all over the country and they were slowly changing over to motorbikes. In 1938 there were 1,500 AA motorcycle patrols – but still 860 patrolmen who used pushbikes, which meant that you might have had a long wait at a place like Dunmail Raise. In the 1950s, as AA membership rose to 700,000, motorcycle combinations – with a toolkit and can of spare petrol in the sidecar – were the norm and two-way radios were introduced. This is the heyday of the AA patrolman in the popular imagination, a sort of cross between St Christopher and the Good Samaritan in his paramilitary uniform of khaki jacket and blue trousers, his badges, medals and stripes, his cheery smile and his predilection for saluting every oncoming car sporting that iconic bulging badge of intertwined As and a pair of wings.

The boring square badge came in 1967, and with it a less glamorous service. Motorbikes were phased out in favour of Minivans and Austin Minor Vans – and even, in a single case, a Reliant Regal, such as Del Boy drove in *Only Fools and Horses*. In the 1970s and 1980s the road-side boxes were replaced by utilitarian metal cabinets attached to posts, but now, in the age of the mobile phone, even these have gone. The quaint little kiosks that remain are categorised as listed buildings now, so they can't be sold or removed. Instead they fulfil the pleasing function of reminding us of an era when motoring had a sense of innocence and adventure about it.

At the beginning of the 1950s just 13 per cent of British households had access to a car, which made the public roads a privileged playground for the minority who did.

And the byways of the Lake District were ideal, reckoned Christopher Trent, the author of *Motoring Holidays in Britain*: 'most of the roads are well surfaced and though many of the minor ones are narrow, twisting and have many steep hills, there is nothing to deter the average motorist, whatever the age of his car, provided that it has good brakes and its driver is prepared to go slowly where the ways are narrow.'

The car, indeed, was an excellent thing all round, for it brought new prosperity to the region. 'Catering for holiday-makers is . . . the chief industry of this part of Cumberland and Westmorland,' wrote Trent. 'It is an industry which reached its peak fifty or more years ago, when Wordsworth had brought to the Lakes a popularity previously undreamed of and one which has been revived in the modern era of motoring.'

Fifty years later, of the 11 million annual visitors to Cumbria and the Lakes, 93 per cent arrive by private car, motorbike or motorhome and almost all of them will continue to use their vehicles to get around rather than taking advantage of the excellent public transport network. The result is that many roads, especially the tourist hotspots in and around Windermere, Bowness and Grasmere and the A591, our road of choice, are often nose to tail with traffic. It's a state of affairs that frustrates Richard Leafe, the Chief Executive of the Lake District National Park. 'In the fifties it would have been a lovely place to drive around,' he agrees, 'but now on a bank holiday and in busy periods during the summer it's far from that. We're keen to encourage people to come to the Lake District, but ideally without a car. If they can leave their car at home, come on public transport and enjoy the park by walking out into some of the remoter areas, all the better.'

The issue of how people get here, and in what numbers, has been a thorny question since the earliest days of tourism. Wordsworth, having written a *Guide to the Lakes*, which first appeared in 1810, as well as a body of great poetry that was almost exclusively inspired by these surroundings, appeared horrified later in life when increasing numbers of people decided to come and see for themselves what all the fuss was about. In 1844, when he was 74 years old and Poet Laureate, a new company called the Kendal and Windermere Railway announced plans to build a line right into Bowness, just down the road from Rydal Mount where he was then living in some grandeur. It would then be only a matter of time, Wordsworth felt, before another line was built linking Windermere and Keswick, and this would run past his house and through his beloved Vale of Grasmere. Fearing invasion from the great unwashed of the northern industrial towns, Wordsworth dashed off a sonnet ('Is then no nook of English ground secure/ From rash assault?') and threw himself into a campaign against the proposed railway.

In two long letters to the local *Morning Post* he made his case against what he called 'the Advance of the Ten Thousand . . . We should have the whole of Lancashire, and no small part of Yorkshire, pouring in upon us to meet the men of Durham, and the borderers from Cumberland and Northumberland. Alas, alas, if the lakes are to pay this penalty for their own attractions!' he wrote. 'Hypocrite!' was the general reaction. Having been almost singlehandedly responsible for the fame and popularity of the lakes, he was abhorring the monster he had created. In fact, thanks to Wordsworth's protests, no line from Bowness to Keswick was ever built, but the railway did come to Bowness, and Wordsworth was made to look like a reactionary Canute figure, trying to stem the tide of both technical and social progress.

But Wordsworth was to have the last laugh, or at least mild harrumph. In his *Guide to the Lakes* he had described the Lake District (ironically, given his later views on the railway) as 'a sort of national property, in which every man has a right and an interest who has an eye to perceive and a heart to enjoy'. This notion of common ownership of Britain's rare and beautiful locations inspired a handful of enlightened philanthropists who foresaw the need to protect such places. In 1883, 33 years after Wordsworth's death, Canon Rawnsley – the man who scrabbled around collecting bits of blown-up rock – founded the Lake District Defence Society, with a formidably eggheaded and influential membership that included the poets Alfred, Lord Tennyson and Robert Browning, the critic John Ruskin and the very rich Duke of Westminster.

It was at this time that Rawnsley met the young

Beatrix Potter and instilled in her a lifelong love of Lakeland, and the need to be vigilant in protecting it. In 1895 Canon Rawnsley – along with two others, Octavia Hill and Sir Robert Hunter – founded the National Trust, of which Beatrix Potter would become the first life-member, using the income from her books to support the Trust's projects and campaigns. Seven years later – perhaps mindful of the failure of the Thirlmere Defence Association to stop the reservoir – Rawnsley started a fund-raising campaign to save a tract of land on the shore of Derwentwater, next to Keswick, which property developers wished to build houses on. All sorts of people contributed, from Princess Louise, the daughter of Queen Victoria, to a man in Sheffield who sent 2s. 6d. and a note: 'All my life I have longed to see the Lakes... I shall never see them now, but I should like to help keep them for others.' This land, called Brandelhow, became the first park to be bought by the National Trust. In 1913 Rawnsley bagged Castlerigg Stone Circle for the Trust, just in case someone tried to turn it into a leisure centre.

The Lake District was in safe hands. Since 1951 it has been a National Park – one of 14 in Britain that include Loch Lomond and The Trossachs, the North York Moors and Snowdonia – which has a remit 'to conserve and enhance the [area's] natural beauty, wildlife and cultural heritage'.

When you see those first views of the Vale of Grasmere from the south side of Dunmail Raise, it is hard not to agree with Wordsworth that building a railway line through here would have been a desecration. It is, wrote Thomas West in *A Guide to the Lakes* (1778), 'one of the sweetest landscapes that art ever attempted to imitate... all is peace, rusticity, and happy poverty, in its neatest, most becoming attire.' Not so much has changed – the road we are on is no longer a track, there are a few more buildings in the village and the poor but blissful peasants have mysteriously disappeared, probably driven out by the lack of affordable housing. But essentially we are looking at the same, apparently miniature scene as West gazed on – the tantalising silver fragment of Grasmere itself, the emerald green meadows, gentle fells and billowing woodland lying in the valley haze like so much fluff in Lakeland's belly button.

In her intimate account of life here at the beginning of the nineteenth century, Wordsworth's sister Dorothy is always making pies, shelling peas and doing things to pike. Dove Cottage, which she and William (and, from 1802, William's wife, Mary) occupied between 1799 and 1808, looks so damned cute it could belong to Benjamin Bunny or Tom Kitten, the creations of a very different Lakeland writer. The white, lime-washed walls and small lattice windows are immediately recognisable from the earliest-known painting of the cottage, on display in the Wordsworth Museum next door. Inside, the downstairs is still panelled from when it was a pub (the Dove and Olive Bough) in the eighteenth century. The kitchen utensils and furniture have an air of recent use about them and,

n the study upstairs, the diamond-shaped chair with
curved support in which Wordsworth would sit composing
– his back resting on one side, his notebook on the
other – begs to be sat in (but you're not allowed, so don't).

The place is tiny – three up and three down – dingy, and
hugely atmospheric. For a handful of years at the
beginning of the 1800s, Wordsworth's high-minded and
hippyish circle lived and loved in each other's pockets,
mostly in these half-dozen rooms. Coleridge – who slipped
down from Keswick for trysts with Sara Hutchinson, the
sister of Mary Wordsworth – would sleep in front of the
hearth in the study, while Thomas De Quincey, who took
over the lease of the cottage in 1808, kipped down in the
woodshed. That circular burn mark on the wooden
landing? Maybe it's where De Quincey left a bucket of
burning coals, after over-indulging in the local prepara-
tion of opium known as Kendal Black Drop. A phial of the
stuff – to which Coleridge was also partial – sits in a
display cabinet, alongside Wordsworth's John Lennon-
type sunglasses.

But it's the work that was written here that is most
important. Aided and abetted by Samuel Taylor
Coleridge, Wordsworth produced some of the most
memorable poetry in the English language – including
Ode: Intimations of Immortality, *The Leech-Gatherer*
and his autobiographical epic *The Prelude*, not to
mention something about daffodils – during the few
heady years he spent here. As he explained in the preface
to the *Lyrical Ballads*, he broke new ground in poetry

by showing that 'delicacy and depth of feeling are not limited to any one class of men or women', using incidents and situations from common life. Peasants, recluses, madmen, pedlars, beggars and outcasts whom he heard about and encountered in the surrounding landscape all feature in the poetry of this time. And in writing about them he also expressed the true, sometimes frightening splendour of the fells and lakes, most memorably in *The Prelude*. The journals that Dorothy kept during these years, which paint a detailed and intimate picture of people and places, also reveal the debt that Wordsworth's poetry owes to her acute observations of nature.

But the most vivid, and hilariously rude, physical portrait of the man himself – the stuff about his peculiar legs, and a nose 'existing centuries ago amongst some of the lowest amongst the human species' – is by De Quincey, who was scarcely an oil painting himself. In 1824, in the *John Bull Magazine and Literary Recorder*, an anonymous satirist described the author of *Confessions of an English Opium-Eater*, which had been published three years before, as 'an animal about five foot high . . . with a comical sort of indescribable body, and a head of most portentous magnitude . . . As for the face, its utter grotesqueness and inanity is totally beyond the reach of the pen to describe.' They didn't believe in breaking things gently in those days.

Despite the coaches disgorging tourists at Dove Cottage, such is the allure of this place that it's very possible to feel as though De Quincy and friends are still around here, somewhere. And that if you keep your eyes peeled you might just catch sight of Thomas turning left, around a corner, where once in an opium dream he saw, in place of the Grasmere fells, 'the domes and cupolas of a great city – an image or faint abstraction, caught perhaps in childhood from some picture of Jerusalem'. Resuming our journey south on the A591, which hugs the edge of Grasmere Lake and passes through mixed woodland to Rydal Water, we are just in time to see the raddled and randy opium-eater disappearing into an old cottage tucked beneath the rocky forehead of Nab Scar and facing the lake.

This is the Nab, or Nab Cottage, and it was the home of a farmer's teenage daughter called Margaret Simpson, whom De Quincey was in the habit of visiting in secret, often at night. He eventually got her pregnant and married her (in that order) and they lived together in the Nab, which is one of the most mysterious and beautiful of all the old cottages in Lakeland. It is a long, whitewashed building with a slate roof and pointed stone mullion windows. And on a diamond-shaped lozenge above the porch is an inscription, arranged vertically, that could be some lost alchemical formula and seems in keeping with the oddly occult feel of the place:

I
3P
A
1702

According to Baddeley in the 1909 edition of *The Thorough Guide*, this in fact stands for 'Isaac & Ann Pattinson', who presumably extended the cottage at that date, as it's older than that. After the De Quinceys, Coleridge's son, Hartley, lived here and it is now a guesthouse and a language school. Between the Nab and the lake, the A591 curves on a blind bend that the Triumph takes slowly as we peer at that odd inscription and look for signs of bedroom curtains being closed.

Round the edge of Rydal Water the road rises, falls and twists, and the little Triumph feels like a fairground ride as we work the gears between second, third and fourth. This is just a gentle workout for what's about to follow. A couple of miles south of Rydal we barely kiss the walkers' town of Ambleside before branching steep left off a mini roundabout signposted 'Kirkstone 3'. This narrow, twisting lane is Smithy Brow and it is almost immediately a second-gear job. A red sign warns what's ahead: 'The Struggle. Kirkstone Pass. 1,500 feet. Winter conditions can be dangerous.'

The Kirkstone Pass is not the steepest road pass in Britain – that distinction belongs to another Lakeland pass, Hardknott, where the gradient reaches 1:3 – but it is probably the highest and was certainly grim and gruelling for the travellers who used it before mechanised transport. Today the road is still as challenging as the remote track it once was, twisting, steep and treacherous in bad weather.

In the Triumph it's necessary to stay in second as the

road climbs clear of Ambleside between drystone walls, twists and turns, flattens out and goes downhill at one point. Over to the right, the east, the sloping fellsides have been drawn on by the straight pencil lines of drystone walls. We climb up into cloud and those stone walls to either side seem suddenly higher, as if we are struggling the wrong way – oops, we crunch down into first and the TR3A shudders and jolts – up a bobsleigh chute.

We are now climbing so slowly it would almost be possible to reach out and pluck handfuls of the pale grasses and bracken that line the roadsides. Looming through the swirling cloud, a crow sits dead still, like a sinister harbinger, on the top of the wall. Then the cloud clears a little and the twinkling lights of the Kirkstone Pass Inn become visible through the gloom, blazing as brightly as if it were late evening, though it is scarcely midday. The road descends again – we even manage to get the Triumph up into third – past sheep grazing on verges, then we change down into first for the final ascent up a gradient that hits 1:4 on a series of switchbacks. All the while, the roofline of the inn is just visible. This was the final struggle for weary packhorses and travellers, and their reward of hay and ale would have been tantalisingly and inspiringly in sight for a good quarter-hour before they reached the top of the pass.

The road we meet is the A592, which runs between Windermere to the south and Penrith in the north and which we shall presently be following towards Penrith.

But first we have urgent business across the road in the inn. 'Here the road, or "struggle", from Ambleside comes in,' says Baddeley in the old *Thorough Guide*, 'and everybody, man and beast, stops for a "refresher".' The inn is a medieval building and used to be called the Traveller's Rest. It catered for itinerant workers, such as the ancient and spooky leech-gatherer whom Wordsworth met not far from here, for until the advent of tourism in the late 1700s these were the only kind of people needing lodging in the Lake District.

We push open the ancient wooden door with its curious rounded corners, and walk into a low-ceilinged, beamed bar with slate and granite flooring and a fire flickering in the grate. A figure sits warming himself in front of the fire and staring contemplatively into its embers. Wordsworth may well have written a poem about John Jennings, had he met him. John was born into a poor but close-knit community in east London in 1949, 'when there were still ships in the docks, and bombed-out houses with no windows or roofs'. He has done a deal of this and that in his life – local government surveyor, estate agent, businessman, publican – and four years ago happened to walk through the door we have just closed behind us. He and his wife, Gail, had come up to the Lakes to attend a Buddhist retreat and popped in to the Kirkstone Inn because when you see it that's what you feel compelled to do.

'I was fourteen when I left the Isle of Dogs and I never felt at home again till I walked through that door,' he says. 'It spoke to us. It said, "Help." It was a spiritual thing.'

When they discovered the inn was for sale, they decided to buy it, despite the fact that they didn't, as a general rule, like pubs. That was the easy bit – they would turn it into the kind of pub that they *would* like – so music (except the live variety), televisions and swearing were consigned to the bleak fellsides. 'I can do that in my little patch,' he says. 'This is my bat, my ball and my wicket.' And so a Lakeland institution was preserved.

We borrow a jug of water from behind the bar to fill up the Triumph's radiator after the exertions of the Struggle, and when we return it, John looks up from his place by the fire, and says, ominously: 'There are suggestions that what was here is still here,' he says. 'If you're sensitive.' Time to leave.

Man and vehicle being thoroughly refreshed we turn north on to the A592. Within a hundred yards, we reach the high point of the Kirkstone Pass – the Kirk Stone itself, a monolith with a roof-shaped top, is on the fellside to the left – and begin the descent towards Ullswater. The cloud lifts sufficiently for us to see the long, twisting views down the valley, with the fells falling to either side like woolly green and brown knuckles. And cradled at the point of perspective is the glinting fragment of Brothers Water, surrounded by emerald green flood meadows.

Despite going downhill, we are still stuck in second – a sign warns that the gradient is 20% – 1:5 – and advises 'Low gear for 1¾ miles'. The lack of speed is no bad thing. We have the road to ourselves, and time to admire the views and appreciate the colours: the brown bracken, the pale yellows and greens of the grasses, the flannel-grey of the rock, green-grey of the drystone walling and blue-grey of the scree. The wind-blasted branches of thorn trees are swept back like gelled hair. There is a curious sense of existing in two seasons or climates at once – ahead of us the fellside is patched with sunlight, while cloud still swirls round our little Triumph.

We edge down in a series of S-bends, past Brothers Water and the Brotherswater Inn, to the valley bottom. A crocodile of walkers heads for Helvellyn, which is now on our left. A group of mountain-bikers pedals the other way. The cloud is suddenly back in its rightful place, high above us, and the sun really is shining down here. We have landed in a miraculously green and tranquil spot.

It's so glorious it's necessary to stop and fold back the soft top, and just as we set off again, a tractor pulls out from a field directly in front of us. As the cars behind fall into an obedient line, like ducklings, it feels like a temporary reassertion of priorities. The roads and fells of the Lake District belonged to the leech-gatherers and shepherds, long before the guidebook-toting tourists and walkers arrived. The sheep farmers who continue to eke out an increasingly difficult living from the valleys and uplands of the Lakes are also the custodians of the landscape – as well as tending the sheep, without which no portfolio of Lakes photographs would be complete, they mend the drystone walls, maintain the footpaths, and drive their tractors very slowly on narrow roads.

This one turns left past the red telephone box, where a

sign indicates Deepdale Hall Farmhouse Bed and Breakfast, and we follow him up a bumpy track – taking it slow in the low-slung Triumph – to one of these long, low, whitewashed farmhouses that seem to be hunkering down in the landscape against some cataclysmic future event of which only they have knowledge. The fells behind are among the most majestic in the Lakes, sweeping up in a series of funnels and gullies to the Helvellyn range of mountains.

The tractor driver's name is Chris Brown. He and his son Jimmy run this remote fell farm between them, supplementing their income with a couple of self-catering units in a converted barn. The farm has been in their family since 1954 – 'Fifty-four years,' says Chris. 'I don't know whether we'll do another fifty-four though,' he says gloomily over mugs of tea in the Aga-warmed farmhouse kitchen. Farmers, he admits, are naturally lugubrious creatures, but that is understandable in a world in which they feel increasingly out of step. Sheep farming in these high places is one of the few ways of life that essentially – bar the odd quadbike – hasn't changed since the Vikings came here in the eighth century, reputedly bringing with them the hardy Herdwick sheep that continue to be the mainstay of the Lakeland flocks. It is solitary work. Chris and Jimmy have 600 sheep – mostly Swaledales, with about 100 Herdwick – and a few cattle, and look after 166 acres of walled land and 2,000 acres of Deepdale Common, of which they graze a third. From the perspective of these immutable fells, the rapidly changing world outside can seem increasingly crazy. And times are increasingly tough.

The foot and mouth outbreak of 2001 was a disaster for everyone in the Lake District. To prevent the disease being spread, the fells were declared out of bounds, which effectively posted a 'Closed until further notice' sign in the window of the entire region. From February until the beginning of August footpaths, cafés, hotels, youth hostels and outdoor-clothing shops were dead to the world. But it was particularly hard for the farmers living in remote valleys like Deepdale. Not only did they have to see their livestock being taken away and possibly slaughtered – in the event, Deepdale's were saved – but they saw hardly a soul from week to week. Chris remembers going up the high valley after the footpaths had been closed. It had snowed and was eerily beautiful, with no humans or their footprints to be seen. But they soon grew miserable and lonely. 'A lot of people have the impression that farmers are hard, grumpy people that shout "Get off my land!"' says Jimmy. The truth was they missed the human companionship, as well as the income, of the tourists and were moved to tears by the plight of the animals.

Foot and mouth was a brutal lesson in just how fragile this most ruggedly beautiful and independently minded of English regions really is. Now the problem is purely economic. 'The cost of producing outweighs the price we get for our product,' says Jimmy, for whom the golden age of sheep farming in the fells harks back to a time before tourists, before mechanisation and before proper roads.

'In 1720,' he says, 'the price of wool was more than twice what we get for it now.'

'At the same time, the stuff we buy in for feeding the sheep has doubled in price,' says Chris. 'Fertiliser has almost doubled. But what we get stays the same. There's a lot of farms disappeared here and amalgamated. So you lose some of the community. And the houses are let out to someone not involved in farming.'

'"Affordable housing",' chips in Jimmy contemptuously. It's a buzzword used by politicians. It means "unaffordable". Local people on their wages – minimum wages, perhaps – can't afford them. All the local houses go for extortionate prices for people to live in three weeks of the year. It affects everything – schools, post offices, sports teams. My football team, Ullswater United, only has a handful of locals in it.'

'It's more multinational than Chelsea,' confirms Chris, who then cheers up a bit. Their 'diversification' (another piece of officialese) into tourism with the self-catering units enables them to make ends meet, and maybe things weren't so different in the 1950s. 'Fifty years ago people would be farming here, but they'd also be working in the lead mine,' he says. 'People have always had something else to keep the wolf from the door.'

The lead mine in question is the Greenside mine, which closed in 1962. But maybe that wasn't such an attractive fallback. In 1952 four men died of carbon monoxide poisoning at Greenside. Orchestrating guests' cooked breakfasts on the Aga seems less hazardous. Greenside mine – which Baddeley, in *The Thorough Guide*, called 'The one blot' on the area's 'otherwise almost perfect loveliness' – is a couple of miles north of Deepdale Farm, in a valley of scree and rocky outcrop. Where that valley opens out into the southernmost tail of Ullswater, William Wordsworth had the fright of his young life.

The A592 takes us right there, past a sign that says 'Caution. Red squirrels crossing', with a cute picture of a red squirrel on it, through the straggling cottages of Patterdale village, and into Glenridding. Beyond the steamer pier and the Glenridding Hotel, the road runs up against the shoreline of the lake and a sign warns of falling rocks for 250 yards. Twisting along the edge of the lake in this little red sporty number, with a rock face looming to our left, it feels momentarily as if we are zipping along some Mediterranean corniche in a fifties rom com. But in place of Brigitte Bardot, Wordsworth himself materialises in the passenger seat, gesticulating frantically at that inland rock. 'This was the one,' he mouths over the roar of the two-litre engine as the sound bounces off the rock. The rock is Stybarrow Crag, 'a lofty mountain, deeply scarred by winds and torrents, with oaks growing out of its interstices', according to yet another nineteenth-century guidebook writer, John Robinson. But actually, as Wordsworth found out, it's not really a mountain at all.

Even as a child, Wordsworth would moon about poetically at all times of day and night. As he recounts in *The Prelude*, on one occasion he was mooching by

The Lake District

Writer Hunter Davis and I beside breathtaking and restful Crummock Water.

camera car filming me driving down the Kirkstone Pass near Ambleside, Cumbria. Look out for the camera poking out of the roof.

The Kirkstone Pass, above Ambleside in the Lake District – one of Britain's highest road passes and a true challenge in a fifties manual car!

The M6 at Penrith is a roaring streak of modernity on the edge of the peaceful Lake District.

With the Austin Cambridge in the lush Forest of Dean. Such a pretty c

Tintern Abbey. Grand and picturesque, even with scaffolding!

The Trossachs

A very grand
homecoming.
Visiting my
sister Moira in
my home town
of Greenock.

ge bikes –
d bikers –
utside the
rig o'Turk
earoom in
Trossachs.
e're about
o do one of
favourite
rides, the
ke's Pass.

Silver shadow...
Loch Katrine,
in its enigmatic
glory, and
the venerable
Bentley
Mark VI.

With tour
guide Hugh
O'Neil sailing
Loch Katrine
on the *Sir
Walter Scott*.

Driving p
stunning
Loch Ard

The Bentley
reaches the
end of the road
at Inversnaid.
'All that one
hears is the
ticking of the
cooling engine.'

moonlight at this end of Ullswater when he found a rowing boat tied to a tree inside a cave and decided to 'borrow' it. The second largest lake in the Lake District, after Windermere, Ullswater has a remote and sinuous beauty that the low-key tourism on its shores has never threatened to compromise. In the course of describing this episode, Wordsworth paints a delicately beautiful picture of the patterns left on the surface of the water as the boat moves forward: 'Leaving behind her still, on either side/ Small circles glittering idly in the moon/ Until they melted all into one track/ Of sparkling light.'

As he rows further into the middle of the lake, he takes his bearings from Stybarrow Crag. And suddenly, from behind the crag as he stares at it, 'a huge peak, black and huge/ As if with voluntary power instinct/ Upreared its head', scaring the living daylights out of him. He starts to row frantically away but this *thing* – in fact the summit of Glenridding Dodd, behind Stybarrow Crag – seems to follow him. Frightened and confused, he returns the boat to its mooring place and for days afterwards he can't get the image of this malevolent shape out of his head as it morphs into 'huge and mighty forms, that do not live/ Like living men'. Of course, it is always possible that Glenridding Dodd is the gentlest of giants and that, awoken from its timeless slumbers, it was as frightened of this intense and strangely put-together young boy as the boy was of it.

It is hard, on a sunny afternoon, to read malevolence into the Ullswater scene. The road curves along the lake with only drystone wall dividing the two. The choppy waters break in wavelets on the shoreline. We ignore the left turn to Dockray, Matterdale and Troutbeck and follow the other cars into the National Trust car park for Aira Force. The Lake District's many waterfalls pulse with the power of the fells and there couldn't be a more appropriate name for them than the Old Norse word 'force'.

There are higher and wider falls than Aira Force, which is wedged into a wooded gorge on the north shore of Ullswater, but none has Aira's parkland setting and high and low viewing points, in the form of flint bridges at the head and foot of the falls itself. The lower bridge faces the 65-foot high falls head on, while the upper arch has vertiginous views of the water pumping down through its tunnel of smooth, glistening rocks in a cloud of vapour.

It's well worth pausing awhile here, watching and listening to the waters tumbling and roaring through this damp chasm and into the tea-coloured waters below. For soon, too soon, we shall be meeting an entirely different kind of tumult and cacophony. With this in mind, we slow to a reluctant crawl for the rest of the way. After Aira Force, the road passes through Gowbarrow Park, another National Trust acquisition, where, in 1802, Wordsworth saw the daffodils at the water's edge that inspired his most famous lines. On the far side of the lake, the foreshore is lined with trees and the bracken-covered fellsides rise steeply behind. After several miles of undulating road that both hugs and pushes away from the lake at different points, we reach the sign we had hoped not to see, for a while longer anyway: the one pointing to the future – only it doesn't say 'The Future', of course. It says: 'M6 5 miles'. Five miles later, approaching Junction 40 of the M6, the Penrith intersection, we pass beneath a digital information board that says: 'M6 junctions 18, 19 long delays'. Naturally.

Britain's first stretch of motorway, the Preston bypass (now part of the M6 and the M55), was opened by the Prime Minister, Harold Macmillan, on 5 December 1958. On the same day, incidentally, the STD telephone system, enabling long-distance calling without the need to go through an operator, was inaugurated by the Queen when she rang Edinburgh from Bristol and ordered a new corgi.

The Preston bypass was the first 8.26 miles of a national motorway network that has grown to more than 2,000 miles, with Ms all the way from 1 to 90. In 1958, only those few who had travelled abroad, to the USA, Germany (*vielen dank*, Adolf) or Italy (*grazie*, Benito), had actually seen a motorway. But Britain's antiquated roads, which in most cases were merely metalled versions of cart tracks, needed bringing into the age of the car.

'It's doleful to realise that when completed the Preston by-pass will be the first major road built in Britain since the Roman era,' wrote the author of the *Daily Mail Motoring Guide 1958*. The official brochure for the opening of the bypass explained helpfully that 'The national motorways are designed to enable traffic to travel safely at high speeds, and to minimise the chance of accidents arising from bad driving.' They were to be

laid out in such a way that 'the absence of long lengths of straight road and the variety and treatment of the bridges will prevent the boredom which is sometimes reported as occurring on foreign motorways.' Good heavens, we couldn't be doing with foreign boredom. Let's make our own and call it the Watford Gap.

One year after the opening of the Preston bypass, the first 60-mile stretch of the M1 was opened, including the Watford Gap service area, which, as well as being the general butt of jokes, soon became a useful byword for the dividing line between the North and the South. A year after that, the Triumph TR3A was manufactured in Coventry. Fast and stylish, with excellent braking, it was the perfect car for taking advantage of the new, still relatively empty motorways that were being planned and built throughout the country in the 1960s. Nowadays, the shores of Ullswater suit her just fine.

Chapter 5

The Wye Valley & Forest of Dean

Old Aust Ferry terminal – M48 across Severn Bridge to Chepstow – A466 to Monmouth – A4136 into Forest of Dean – unclassified road from Mitcheldean to Littledean then Blakeney – A48, then first right back into the Forest, on unclassified roads to Speech House – left on B4226 to Hopewell Colliery – continue on B4226 to B4432 – right turn to Symond's Yat Rock crossing A4136

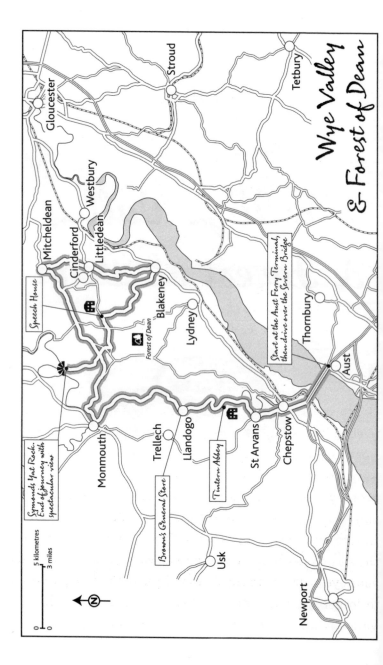

Wye Valley
& Forest of Dean

Stroud

Tetbury

Start at the Aust Ferry Terminal,
then drive over the Severn Bridge.

Gloucester

Mitcheldean

Westbury

Cinderford

Littledean

Speech House

Blakeney

Forest of Dean

Lydney

Thornbury

Aust

Symonds Yat Rock.
End of journey with
spectacular view

Monmouth

Trellech

Llandogo

Tintern Abbey

St Arvans

Chepstow

Brown's General Store

Usk

Newport

5 kilometres
0
3 miles
0

N

The Wye Valley & Forest of Dean

IT FEELS LIKE A REWARD AFTER driving the tin corridor that is the M4, with its inevitable clog-ups around Heathrow and the M25 and the lorry that always seems to shed its load just before you reach Swindon: the Severn Road Bridge. Elegant and even beautiful in its own right – try looking at it from the Welsh side on a bright summer evening: the towers turn a pearlescent white in the low sun – it brings light and promise after the grim slog west. In fact, it is two bridges – the first spanning the Severn, the second the River Wye – and as you speed across it and your eye is drawn to the distant Brecon Beacons, it is easy to forget what lies directly beneath your tyres: the Wye Valley in all its meandering beauty and rich history.

Time was that the Wye Valley was not only pretty, it was also pretty hip. There is a strong case to be made for the stretch between Ross and Chepstow being the birthplace of tourism in Britain. The leisured, the wealthy and the curious – and artists and poets with rock-star cachet, such as J. M. W. Turner and William Wordsworth – began to come here towards the end of the eighteenth century, drawn by a certain quality in the landscape. Its beauty, yes, but also a thrilling wildness. And they came clutching the same book: *Observations on the River Wye, and Several Parts of South Wales, &c, Relative Chiefly to Picturesque Beauty: Made in the Summer of the Year 1770*, by the artist and vicar William Gilpin, with aquatint illustrations by his nephew.

This leather-bound pocket book (not actually published till 1783) was the first of several 'tours' Gilpin wrote up of various British landscapes. In as much as they inspired British people to experience and enjoy their own countryside, rather than seeking inspiration abroad, these books can be said to be the first modern guidebooks. And Gilpin started right here.

The beauty of the Wye Valley, which is now protected by its designation as an Area of Outstanding Natural Beauty, is undimmed from Gilpin's days. Its serpentine course and steep wooded sides, its craggy lookouts – Eagle's Nest, Devil's Pulpit, Lover's Leap – and stereophonic birdsong, seem to exist in a different dimension from the modern world.

The hotels, bed and breakfasts and campsites testify to

the Wye's enduring popularity with tourists. Just a few miles to the east, wedged between the Severn estuary and the ancient earthwork of Offa's Dyke – built in the eighth century by the English King Offa to keep the Welsh where he could see them – lies an altogether more mysterious and secretive terrain. Still heavily wooded, riddled with old mine workings and governed by laws passed down from Norman times, the Forest of Dean is England's strangest, most remote corner, where people indulge in practices that sound as if they should be illegal – sheep badgering for one.

Just a few miles but a wealth of stories – so let's step on it, and trust that the Austin Cambridge A55 Mark I – so perfectly and palely green it looks like a block of pistachio ice cream – can handle it. But if we follow the 1950s guidebooks, we'll be a long time arriving. According to a booklet published by the Wye Valley and the Royal Forest of Dean Tourist Board, 'Travellers by car will find that the Severn crossing by the Aust–Beachley ferry will save a detour of some fifty miles.' In fact, the old ferry stopped running on 8 September 1966 – the day the first Severn Road Bridge (there's now a second one) opened, and the first episode of the first series of *Star Trek* was broadcast on American television.

There had been some sort of ferry service between Aust (on the Somerset side of the estuary) and Beachley (in Gloucestershire but near the Welsh border) since medieval times. In 1725 Daniel Defoe, the author of *Robinson Crusoe*, referred to the crossing as 'ugly, dangerous, and very inconvenient' in *A Tour Through the Whole Island of Great Britain,* one of the early and great travel books. Ugly and dangerous it may have been then, but it certainly wasn't inconvenient, for the alternative was to travel all the way up to Gloucester, cross the Severn there, and journey back down – a round trip of some 60 miles and a lifetime of journeying in those days. Even so, Defoe, perhaps wary of getting his wig wet, took the road option.

The modern service had started in the 1920s and in August 1931 a car-and-passenger ferry was inaugurated by the Old Passage Severn Ferry Co. Ltd, owned by one Enoch Williams. By the time of the ferry's closure in 1966, there were three boats plying this mile-long route: the *Severn King, Severn Queen* and *Severn Princess.* The fare for foot passengers was one shilling, for 'juvenile passengers' sixpence, and for a car and driver nine and six – and there was a snack bar on Beachley Pier called the Quickie. The more innocent times in which such a name could be spoken with a straight face are long gone, but there are fascinating remnants of the ferry itself.

Coming from the east, even some of the old road signs for the Aust Ferry are still in place, if you look hard enough. There's one in Bristol (with the word 'Ferry' painted out) and there's one on the B4461 to the east of the city, pointing to Chipping Sodbury one way and Aust Ferry the other. But the easiest way to find the old pier is to come off the M48 (as the Severn Road Bridge is now designated) at Junction 1, follow the A403 south towards

Avonmouth for a short distance, then turn right at the signpost for St Augustine's Vineyard into Passage Road. After a mile, following a descent, there is a sharp right-hand turn marked only by a dead-end sign. As you come to an uncertain halt by the gate at the end of this lane and gaze at the derelict, pebbledashed, one-storey building behind the chainlink fence, you may, if your imagination is particularly vivid and you are, perhaps, of a certain age, feel some vague stirrings of recognition. Or you may just swear at your satnav and prepare to reverse out and look elsewhere.

But that would be hasty. The scene may have changed utterly, but this is the spot where the great Bob Dylan – the singer–songwriter and rock 'n' roll revolutionary whose words and music shaped new ways of looking at the modern world – stood and scowled his way into photographic iconography on a rainy day in May 1966 – 11 May to be precise. Dylan was on his way to play a gig in Cardiff, having played the Colston Hall in Bristol the night before. This was the world tour in which Dylan and his backing band, The Hawks (which became The Band), dared to play deafening, electric rock 'n' roll – and the audience of baffled folkies got their sandals in a twist. Six days after he had stood on the pier at Aust, a fan at the Manchester Free Trade Hall would famously denounce him as 'Judas'; the night before, the audience at the Colston Hall had booed and slow-handclapped him, and this, together with the lousy British weather, had put him in a bad mood.

That, at least, is the recollection of the photographer, Barry Feinstein. So there Dylan stands, pipecleaner-thin in his paramilitary jacket, hands thrust deep in jeans pockets, with that nimbus of dark hair, impenetrable, cooler-than-thou shades and inscrutable expression (though he sure ain't having a ball). The stones of the pier are shiny with rain. And in the background is the ghostly outline of the brand-new Severn Road Bridge, not yet opened, which just four months later would put the Aust–Beachley ferry out of business. This photograph, cropped in different ways and copied countless times, is said to be Dylan's favourite of himself and was chosen to promote the 2005 Martin Scorsese film about him, *No Direction Home*.

Slowly, as you look, the image coalesces. You need to screen out the thick margin of reeds that have grown all around the pier, replace the wooden extension of the pier, long since rotted away, and strip the pebbledash from the old wooden terminal building. Luckily, one section of that chainlink fence has been trodden down by determined Dylanologists, so you can go exploring, as many Dylan freaks have evidently done before you. That sheet of sodden A4 caught in the reeds turns out to be a photocopy of Feinstein's picture; and someone has stencilled a head-and-shoulders likeness of Dylan on to the pebbledash. Best of all, you notice that the stones on the pierside are the same as in the foreground of the photo, and that the iron bollard is still there. From that, you can follow the crack in the stone to find the precise spot on which Dylan was standing in his hipster boots. And, to paraphrase the words of 'Positively 4th Street', you can, for just one time, stand inside his shoes.

One Dylan fan who was particularly thrilled to discover where Feinstein's famous photograph was shot is a Chepstow-born folk music and boat fanatic called Tim Ryan. He had seen the image many times before his son called him in a state of high excitement to tell him about the Aust ferry connection. At a stroke, the two enthusiasms of his life became joined at the hip. Youthfully middle-aged, with straggly hair that hints at a hirsute, concert-going youth, Tim pores over the photograph and reads it like runes. The car in the background is an Austin Princess. 'Which is ironic,' says Tim, clutching at the straws of cultural synchronicity, 'because the ferry is the *Severn Princess*.'

He doesn't remember Bob Dylan being in the neighbourhood – in any case, Dylan presumably just sped on to Cardiff – but he does remember the visit of the Beatles to Chepstow at around the same time. 'Our teachers took us up and we watched them going up the high street in their limo,' he says. He also recalls it because it made ferry history – it was the only occasion on which the 'no advance bookings' rule was relaxed, apart from when the Queen and Prince Philip made the crossing in 1957 (in separate ferries of course).

Gazing along the bonnet of the Cambridge at the derelict pier, it is tempting to mourn the passing of the old car ferry. But by the time our modest little saloon, named after a university town, was built, at BMC's Longbridge plant in 1958, the ferry was hopelessly overworked. It had two different names – Aust or Beachley – according to which side of the river you caught it on, and Tim has the old 'Beachley Ferry' sign, which could once be found on the wall of the police station in Tutshill, on the outskirts of Chepstow. He remembers the queue of cars to get on the Beachley Ferry stretching as far back as the sign – two miles.

'The crossing took twelve minutes and the ferry carried nineteen cars – so there's a whole generation of kids my age who know their nineteen times table,' he says, proceeding to recite it. They would be sent forward along the queue of cars by their parents to count in nineteens so they knew approximately how long they would have to wait for the ferry and whether it was worth it. On busy days it was not uncommon to wait two or three hours to get on.

'Health and safety-wise it's laughable what they got away with,' he says. 'There were nineteen cars, ninety-eight passengers and six lifebelts – on the most dangerous river in the country. They would sail with both ramps down and motorbikes on the ramps.' The Severn is indeed a dangerous river, with the second biggest tidal range in the world – up to nearly 50 feet – and treacherous mudflats, but the cars which rode the ferries were never chained down. At Aust in the late 1950s, a sign read: 'When parked in position on the ferry please switch off engine, engage low gear and apply handbrake.' Tim has flickering footage from 1939 which shows old Flatnose Morrises shooting up the ramps and being spun into position on a turntable hand-pulled by rope. The cars were simply packed tight together to stop them moving about. 'You couldn't open the doors,' says Tim. 'Imagine that. You couldn't get out.'

Tim emphasises just what a barrier the Severn was before the opening of the road bridge, culturally and psychologically as well as physically. 'That river was an absolute monster. A real border. [Crossing from the west] it really was like going abroad. I didn't go to Bristol till I was fourteen or fifteen. It was impossible to get to.'

When the road bridge opened on 8 September 1966, it was well received on both sides of the river, not least because in the several years it took to build it had provided much local employment – Tim's father was a welder who worked on the deck sections – and all the ferry workers were found work on it. On that September day Tim and his classmates were given half a day off school and taken down to the bridge approach road where they waved flags while dignitaries, including the Queen, performed the inaugural honours, and locals on this 'Welsh' side – actually still in England – realised the world was now their oyster. 'It opened up the area,' says Tim. 'Exotic places like Weston-super-Mare were suddenly available.'

The ferries that had put in such sterling service went the sad way of old boats: they were broken up or set to work on undignified tasks. The newest, the *Severn*

Princess – built in Hull in 1959 – found employment on the west coast of Ireland, transporting goods between Galway Bay, the Aran Islands and Westport. By the late 1990s she had been made redundant again and this time faced the knacker's yard. That was when Dr Richard Jones – the son of the founding father of the old ferry, Enoch Williams – stepped in to save her and return her to her home of Chepstow. She was towed back from Ireland, pursued by dolphins, and almost sank in a Force Nine off the Mumbles headland in South Wales. But she made it and now lies on the west bank of the Wye, beneath the A48 road bridge. She is rusting and defaced with graffiti, but – after all she has been through – defiant-looking. Richard Jones, Tim Ryan and a team of enthusiasts are slowly renovating her and the plan is that she will take pride of place in a redevelopment of the river frontage – a testament to a slower, simpler age, with that improbable touch of rockstar glamour. After all, it was not every boatman in the 1960s who could say, 'I had that Bob Dylan in the back of the ferry once.'

Though Chepstow is now theoretically plugged into the rest of the world, thanks to the Severn Road Bridge, it still feels rather overlooked. To the south the M48 hurries past, as if eager to merge again with the M4, from which it split on the eastern shore (the M4 spans the estuary some five miles south, on a bridge opened in 1996 called the Second Severn Crossing), and together they speed on towards Cardiff and Swansea. And Chepstow sits, like a boy on a kerbstone, watching the tail lights disappear and wondering whether to splash out on a day trip to the fleshpots of Weston-super-Mare.

The pace of Chepstow feels more B-road than motorway. Not a great deal has happened here, you feel, since its medieval castle was besieged by Parliamentary forces in 1645. The castle, built on limestone cliffs overlooking the Wye, still dominates the town. The kids who congregate on the grassy slopes below its fortifications may have face-rings and baggy trousers, but they are unnervingly polite and respectful of their elders. And no doubt where they now hang out J. K. Rowling once mooched and dreamed of escape, for she lived here. More precisely, the creator of Harry Potter grew up just across the old iron bridge in the suburb of Tutshill, which is in fact in England, whereas Chepstow proper, on the west bank of the Wye, is in Wales. You can see where she might have got her ideas from for the parallel reality of Hogwarts. This is a town on a river that are, both of them, simultaneously barriers and portals to other worlds.

The particular portal we're looking for is the A466, signposted to Monmouth 16 miles away, which can be picked up at Junction 2 of the M48. This bypasses the town, continues north past Chepstow Racecourse and does indeed enter another world. The brown 'Heritage' signs are a clue. They point the way to the Wye Valley and Tintern Abbey – the latter the most important stopping-off point on a tour of the former for the tourists who first came here in the eighteenth century.

Pleasure excursions were started by Dr John Egerton,

the rector of Ross-on-Wye, in about 1745, when he took his friends down the river, for fun and the scenery. Soon a two-day package trip was established in which tourists would hire a boat and boatmen at Ross and stop off to visit the various viewing points, natural features, grottoes and landscaped walks along the riverbanks. Tintern Abbey would have been a highlight of the second day, according to Anne Rainsbury, the curator of Chepstow Museum. This is the world we are about to enter – that of the first tourists, not just the first to come here but the first to visit anywhere in Britain in the spirit we have come to associate with tourism. They came to admire an unfamiliar, exotic landscape, to be able to tell tales of wily bumpkins who spoke funny, and to record it all in notebooks and – the camera not yet having been invented – sketchbooks.

This was upmarket, bespoke tourism – the package tourists and daytrippers came later as transport links improved. 'It wasn't cheap to do, so this wasn't for ordinary people,' explains Anne Rainsbury. 'These were people with leisure, people with money, the time to travel and also the desire to travel because you weren't necessarily doing it for sheer fun. You were in pursuit of something, which was the Picturesque.' Anne is an expert on the movement that developed during the eighteenth century and was popularised by William Gilpin in his *Observations on the River Wye*.

Before the eighteenth century, wild landscapes and mountains were considered unruly and even disgusting –

scarcely a fit subject for even looking at, let alone painting. It was as if exposure to vistas of rocks and grass for any length of time would have us de-evolving back into cavemen. But attitudes began to change as British artists and aesthetes became influenced by seventeenth-century European painters such as Claude Lorrain and Nicolas Poussin, who had painted idealised landscapes according to strict rules. The word Picturesque – literally, 'like a picture' – was adopted to describe this style and Gilpin was one of its earliest and most enthusiastic champions.

'He didn't invent the word, but he was one of the masters of its definition,' says Anne Rainsbury. Gilpin's idea was that a particular landscape, or portion of land-scape, viewed from a certain spot, could be as harmonious and beautiful as a painting. '[His book] told you not only where to go and what to see but how to look at it – as if you were composing a picture, making a picture out of the landscape,' explains Anne.

A clue to the precise whereabouts of this picturebook world we are about to drive through is the old stone wall on your right-hand side as you drive past Chepstow Racecourse towards Tintern and Monmouth. This wall, varying in height and including an old gatehouse with locked gates, runs for several miles, following the road when it bears right at the village of St Arvans and continuing on past another sharp right-hander.

On the other side of the wall for much of the way is the racecourse. It's what lies on the other side of that, between the racecourse and the twisting Wye itself, that is significant. This is, or was, Piercefield Park and in the eighteenth and nineteenth centuries it became as popular as the London Eye is to present-day visitors to the capital because it made accessible the awesome river scenery that previously had only been viewable by boat.

Occupying a promontory of woodland and cliffs wedged into a deep and narrow loop of the Wye, it was a kind of early theme park in that it had been discreetly land-scaped to provide footpaths and viewing points in keeping with the then fashionable principles of the Picturesque. These vantage points – called, variously, Lover's Leap, the Giant's Cave, the Grotto – were situated and designed to be come across suddenly, as if by chance, so the tourist, in that elegant eighteenth-century phrase, would be gobsmacked by the vistas opening up below them – of the Wye itself, of Chepstow Castle on its ridge of limestone cliffs, of the distant Severn estuary.

Piercefield was the brainchild of a white sugar planter and slave owner from Antigua called Valentine Morris. In a curious twist, it was later owned by a West Indian called Nathaniel Wells, the son of a black slave and a white sugar planter from St Kitts. In 1818 Wells became Britain's first black sheriff when he was appointed to that office for the county of Monmouthshire. Sadly, Piercefield as Valentine Morris originally conceived it has pretty much gone the way of the Severn ferry boats. Though the Wye Valley Walk follows the main path through the woodland of Piercefield, the atmosphere is dank and forlorn, with little birdsong. The viewing points have fallen into disrepair – the semi-circular Grotto, built into the side of an iron-age hillfort, once glittered with mineral crystals but is now just a musty hole – and many of the views have been entirely obscured by trees, or offer the merest glimpse of the Wye's glistening mudbanks far below.

The house itself – enlarged and redesigned by Sir John Soane in 1785 – is a roofless ruin, and the spot from which, in 1811, J. M. W. Turner must have sketched his *Junction of the Severn and the Wye* (showing Chepstow Castle, the bend of the Wye below it and the Severn estuary in the distance) is completely overgrown. It is somewhere near Chepstow Leisure Centre, the car park of which is the access point to Piercefield from Chepstow. This modern local amenity, with its swimming pool, sauna and steam rooms and aerobics studio, has entirely eclipsed the visionary eighteenth-century amenity on its doorstep that was dreamed up by Valentine Morris.

Piercefield Park, though it drew on ideas of the Picturesque, was actually designed and opened before Gilpin's *Observations on the River Wye* was published. When Gilpin visited in 1770 he admitted that, 'Mr Morris's improvements at Persfield [sic] . . . are generally thought as much worth a traveller's notice as anything on the banks of the Wye.' But being a sniffy and pompous type – and perhaps miffed that Morris had contrived to create Piercefield without reference to him – he couldn't resist adding that, 'We cannot, however, call these views picturesque. They are either presented from too high a point, or they have little to mark them as characteristic; or they do not fall into such composition as would appear to advantage on canvas.'

Gilpin banged on so much about what and wasn't Picturesque and precisely how things should be looked at that people started to send him up – most notably in one of the satirical poems featuring the mythical Dr Syntax, written by William Coombes and illustrated by the cartoonist Thomas Rowlandson. In *The Tour of Dr Syntax in Search of the Picturesque*, published in 1809, the good doctor promises that, 'I'll ride and write and sketch and print, and thus create a real mint/ I'll prose it here, I'll verse it there, and Picturesque it everywhere/ I'll make this flat a shaggy ridge and o'er the water throw a bridge . . .'

The A466 that follows the course of the river from St Arvans, north of Chepstow, to Monmouth, crossing it on the iron bridge at Bigsweir, wasn't built until the 1820s. Before then the river was the only practicable way to get to these lower reaches of the Wye. There was a road – it crossed the hills to the west, from which lanes descended to various hamlets along the Wye – but it was tough going. In 1746 another travelling vicar, the Revd William Cole – a friend of the Gothic novelist, architect and Member of Parliament, Horace Walpole – described a descent 'through narrow lanes and a most frightful precipice all paved with stone so that your horse can hardly manage himself to get down, much less with anyone on his back'.

The new riverside road revolutionised tourism to the Wye because it coincided with the advent of a steam-packet service from Bristol to Chepstow. Here coaches would meet passengers and whisk them off up the new road for a whistlestop tour of the Wye before delivering them back to the boat, and that evening they'd be back in their villas in Clifton, with the Tintern mud still wet on their boots to prove they'd been so far in a day.

So the A466 is a comparatively new road – and it feels it. It feels like an interloper, as if it exists only provisionally and nature is engaged in a constant battle to oust it. A triangular sign tells you that the tree canopy is only 13 feet above your head; another, pictorial sign warns of the danger of falling rocks from the cliffs on the left-hand side. And a glance up reveals high, forbidding crags draped in mist. 'Reduce speed now' (*Arafwch* in Welsh) exhorts another sign as you descend into Tintern – and then the barrier of vegetation falls away to your right and in its place the empty arches of the abbey windows appear, traceries of stone hanging as if suspended in the limpid valley light.

Tintern Abbey, wrote Gilpin, 'occupies a great eminence in the middle of a circular valley, beautifully screened on all sides by woody hills, through which the river winds its course'. It was founded by Cistercian monks in 1131, grew to Gothic splendour in the thirteenth century and was dissolved in 1536. After that, its sandstone blocks were plundered for building materials, peasants took up residence in its nooks and crannies and ironwork foundries sprang up in the Angidy Valley to the west of it.

It wasn't until the eighteenth century that people began to realise the usefulness of such apparently useless ruins. In the mid-1700s, while Valentine Morris was landscaping Piercefield Park, the Duke of Beaufort, who owned the land, ordered a clean-up of Tintern Abbey. Debris was removed from the interior of the church and the land around it was turfed – but the ivy ('in masses uncommonly large'), mosses and lichens that then covered the stonework remained, much to Gilpin's approval.

Most famously, however, Gilpin frowned upon the 'vulgarity' and excessive 'regularity' of the church's gable ends. 'A mallet judiciously used (but who durst use it?) might be of service in fracturing some of them,' he wrote crossly. A later visitor in the eighteenth century, John Byng, Viscount Torrington, seems to be have been an altogether more cheerful sort. 'The way to enjoy Tintern properly,' he wrote in the *Torrington Diaries*, '. . . is to bring wines, cold meat . . . spread your table in the ruins; and possibly a Welsh harper may be procured from Chepstow.'

What seems amazing now about all these eighteenth and early nineteenth century visitors is that the aspects of Tintern they found disagreeable or which didn't conform to the ideals of the Picturesque were either marginalised or discounted altogether. For this was a very different and less bucolic scene than the one we see today because of the sheer, intrusive scale of industrial activity taking place, not just at Tintern but throughout the Wye Valley from Chepstow to Ross.

There were 22 forges near the abbey – and the stone work is still there, hidden in the undergrowth of the Angidy Valley to the west of the abbey ruins. 'They made masses of iron wire for carding combs, from when we had a woollen industry,' says Anne Rainsbury. 'It wouldn't be idyllic and peaceful because of all the traffic and industry. The lime kilns, the forges, the charcoal being burnt. Trees would have been coppiced. It was a completely different landscape from today, with a different look and feel.'

Yet Turner painted a highly romanticised watercolour of the abbey church in 1794, in which the evening sun is painting the stonework golden and ivy entwines itself over the arches. Wishful and Picturesque thinking, perhaps. Or an enviable ability to see through to the heart of the matter.

Nowadays there are no factories to disturb the peace – but there is an army of Cadw employees (Cadw is the Welsh Assembly's heritage division) tooled up with strimmers and lawnmowers. They insist on carrying on the Duke of Beaufort's good work right next to where you are standing, trying to reflect and enjoy. And there is the scaffolding and green netting, which at any one time seems to be covering some portion of the abbey church.

Time to rummage in the pocket of Turner's breeches for the slim object that no doubt would have been nestling there alongside his copy of Gilpin: a Claude mirror – the secret of his 1794 watercolour, most probably. In the late eighteenth and early nineteenth centuries this convex mirror, backed with black foil and usually oval-shaped, was as popular among devotees of the Picturesque as were Gilpin's guides. It took its name from the French artist Claude Gellée, popularly known as Claude Lorrain, who, in the seventeenth century, painted idealised landscapes framed by a foreground of trees and often featuring ruins and tiny human figures. The idea was that you stood with your back to the scene you wished to look at or paint and framed it in your Claude mirror. The reflection, slightly distorted and drained of detail and colour, had a pleasing painterly quality, and by moving it around you could edit out any unwelcome, non-Picturesque elements. Coloured lenses were available to lend the image a dawn glow, or a ghostly moonlit effect. Pocket-sized, versatile and startlingly effective, the Claude mirror was the digital camera of its day.

As it happens, a Claude mirror is still in use at Tintern. The creation of a Canadian artist called Alex McKay, the three-foot-wide, dark, glass oval stands on a tall pole in the grounds of the Abbey Hotel, facing the abbey ruins across the A466. The reflected image of the abbey, which is viewable online, is eerily beautiful and constantly changing, according to the interplay of clouds and sun. The scaffolding and green netting are blurred into non-existence and the abbey becomes again what Turner painted, and William Wordsworth saw, in the 1790s.

Wordsworth, the Lake poet and *eminence grise* of Romanticism, went one better than Turner – he wrote a poem about Tintern Abbey in which he managed not to mention the abbey at all. *Lines composed a few Miles above Tintern Abbey on revisiting the banks of the Wye during a tour, July 13, 1798* is only 'about' Tintern Abbey in as much as the abbey is mentioned in the title. Neither is the poem 'about' the Wye Valley, except in an idealised way (strictly no industrial grunge). Its subject is about a new and heightened way of thinking, inspired by nature and landscape. It is a sort of manifesto for poetic Romanticism, and in the 200 years since it was written has ensured an enduring parallel fame for the abbey that these bits of old stone might not otherwise have enjoyed.

But if the poem is not strictly about the place, it is very much about what such a place might make you feel and think: how, 'with an eye made quiet by the power/ Of harmony, and the deep power of joy/ We see into the life of things'. It is also, if you believe Wordsworth, an astonishing mental feat.

According to his account, he started writing it in his head while he and his sister Dorothy were on a walking tour of the Wye. On 10 July 1798 they crossed the Severn (unlike Daniel Defoe, they seem to have entrusted themselves to the Aust Ferry) and walked up the valley as far as Goodrich Castle, beyond Monmouth, then back down. He claimed that as he walked he composed and committed to memory the entire poem – 161 lines of extremely tricky stuff – but did not write down a single word till he had returned to Bristol 'after a ramble of four or five days'. It can't have been much fun for Dorothy.

This wasn't Wordsworth's first visit to the Wye – hence the opening lines of the poem: 'Five years have passed; five summers, with the length/ Of five long winters!' He had come here in 1793, on his own, when he had plenty on his plate and on his mind – mainly to do with France. He had just returned from Paris where the French Revolution, which he supported, was at its height and France had declared war on England. He had left behind his lover, Annette Vallon, and their daughter, Caroline, born in 1792, and due to hostilities it would be ten years before he was able to return to see them. Back in England, he was broke and his writing was going nowhere. So, with the world in turmoil and his own life in pieces, he headed to the Wye Valley for some peace and perspective. Five years later he returned, happier and more successful – and this time determined to get a poem out of it.

The poem begins with the poet standing near a waterfall and hearing again 'These waters, rolling from their mountain springs/ With a sweet inland murmur'. The waterfall is real, and you too can stand beside it and understand precisely what he means by that phrase 'sweet inland murmur' – a sound so discreet and distinct from the roar made by seawater. The falls are called Cleddon, and to reach them you take the road signposted 'Trelleck 2½' that branches off the A466 at the village of Llandogo, a couple of miles north of Tintern. Be sure to take the sharp right-hand fork that climbs the steep, heavily wooded escarpment above the west bank of the

Wye and, as it begins to flatten out at the top, turns right at 90 degrees. Next to that bend, in the woods to your left, are the falls – a skein of white water murmuring down between mossy rocks.

A little further along the road from Cleddon Falls, on the right-hand side, is the driveway for Cleddon Hall, a Victorian villa with ornate timbers decorating the eaves. This was once called Ravenscroft and was the birthplace, on 18 May 1872, of the moral philosopher, social reformer and pacifist Bertrand Russell.

His parents, Lord and Lady Amberley, were considered 'forward thinkers', which means they were the sandal-wearing muesli-chompers of their day. In the grounds of Ravenscroft – one likes to think within earshot of the falls where, on a summer's day in 1798, a man started composing in his head one of the greatest and most important poems in the English language – they built a summer-house called Wordsworth's Hermitage where they entertained guests and read aloud from improving works.

More muesli was chomped a couple of miles north – on the opposite riverbank from the A466 – at a medieval house called the Argoed, which in the mid-nineteenth century was owned by Richard Potter, the father of Beatrice Webb. She was a champion of the poor and the co-founder, with her husband Sidney Webb, of the Fabian Society, dedicated to the promotion of socialist ideals. A regular visitor to the Argoed was her fellow Fabian, playwright and turner of memorable quotations, George Bernard Shaw.

As a vegetarian, Shaw would have approved of one o the main local industries – the manufacture of millstones for the grinding of corn. Redbrook, the nearest village to the Argoed, lying on and just to the east of the A466, was also known for its copper, iron and tinplate forges. These works were not relative newcomers, a product of the Industrial Revolution – the first mention of industry at Redbrook was in 1628, when two iron forges were listed and the first commercial copper smelting in Britain took place there at the end of the seventeenth century.

Just like the tin miners in Cornwall, men from Redbrook took their skills in the copper and tinplate works abroad, to Russia, India and Italy. A paradox of apparently parochial villages throughout Britain is that many of their inhabitants once, of necessity, travelled and worked far and wide – in valleys and mountains that would still be considered enviably remote by the leisure travellers of today.

From the Middle Ages to the twentieth century, the men who lived on and near the road between Chepstow and Monmouth were variously skilled in copper and brass smelting, the production of iron, wire and tinplate, in making millstones and paper, and in shipbuilding and brewing. A mid-nineteenth-century engraving of Redbrook, by an unknown artist, shows black smoke streaming from factory chimneys while a group of tourists in a tour boat look on. But this image is very much the exception. As we have seen, painters, writers and journal keepers tended to view the reality of the Wye in the eighteenth and nineteenth centuries through a meta-phorical Claude mirror, excluding what they didn't care for.

When Redbrook's old tinplate works closed in 1961, it was the last factory in Britain making thin tinplate by the traditional method. Since then it is amazing how quickly, and efficiently, man and nature have combined to efface, if not all then most, obvious traces of hundreds of years of toil and attendant dirt. There are ruins dotted about – in the Angidy Valley and at Whitebrook, for example – but many factory buildings and riverside warehouses were knocked down, mills were turned into private houses and the undergrowth has claimed most of the rest, the former activities living on only in local place names: Forge Wood, Furnace Grove, Mill Pond. As a consequence, and as Anne Rainsbury points out, 'The Wye Valley has become much more of a rural idyll now than visitors would have seen in the eighteenth century.'

But, like one of those early and inquisitive tourists, eager to cram in as much as possible, we are getting ahead of ourselves here. Returning to Tintern, let's point the bonnet north past the pubs and hotels that line the road for a mile or so beyond the abbey.

The old Austin Cambridge gets plenty of admiring looks as the road hugs the west bank on a dramatically tight loop of the Wye. The Cambridge Mark I, a successor to the Austin A50, was in production for less than two years, before being superseded by the Mark II with its sharp Italian styling. Yet in that short time some 150,000 were manufactured (they were a snip at £650), a figure that reflects the boom in car ownership in the late 1950s. So there were a lot of Austin Cambridges about in the late 1950s and 1960s, and chances are that the people who stop and stare have their own memories of a Mark I – probably not their own, but their father's, or grand-father's, or family doctor's. Self-effacing in its design, with a surprisingly user-friendly gearshift on the steering column, it's a car that inspires affection.

After that pronounced river loop, the road fades slightly inland to pass Tintern's old railway station, where a ticket hasn't been clipped since the last passenger service ran on 4 January 1959 – the same day on which the Soviet *Luna 1* became the first spacecraft to reach the moon. On that snowy day more than 400 people associa-ted with, or just plain fond of, the Wye Valley line piled on to an eight-coach special at Chepstow, enjoying views of a snowbound Tintern Abbey and being pelted with snowballs by schoolboys on the outskirts of Monmouth.

The waiting room at Tintern is now a café and the signal box an exhibition area, while an old railway carriage nearby is dedicated to the history of the railway that once snaked through the valley.

The Wye Valley line, a single-track branch line between Chepstow and Monmouth, opened in 1876. It was the third means of transport, after the river itself and the road built in the 1820s, by which tourists could visit this part of the Wye. And it was certainly built with day-trippers in mind. But it was also hoped that the various valley industries would make use of it. 'A very great traffic is anticipated from tourists visiting Tintern Abbey,' noted the *Prospectus of the Wye Valley Line*, published in 1874, '. . . and also both in goods and passengers from the resident population, as well as from the quarries, wire works, paper mills, tin-plate works, foundries and other manufactories.'

Unlike the Severn Road Bridge a century later, it was not welcomed by everybody. Farmers feared this fearsome, newfangled intrusion would cause hens to stop laying and cows to stop producing milk, while – surreal as it may seem – the platforms at Chepstow station were denounced as agents of moral turpitude. These platforms were considerably lower than the train carriages, which in the line's first year of operation had led to some undignified scrambling by ladies in armour-plated dresses, and the occasional, inflammatory revelation of female calves. A petition was handed in to the Wye Valley Railway Company, which agreed to raise the level of the platforms in order to prevent the entire Wye Valley being twinned forever with Sodom and Gomorrah. 'It was quite a feat of engineering at the time,' says Anne Rainsbury.

From Chepstow, the line crossed the river twice, at Tintern and Redbrook, thus running both on the Gloucestershire and the Monmouthshire riverbanks, and was regarded as one of the most charming of Britain's rural branch lines. With the glassy waters of the Wye flowing just beyond the carriage windows and the plucky little tank engines, with their round windows and polished brass domes, tooting their way through tunnels of trees – doing their best to put hens off their stroke – it must have been a delight.

By the end of the nineteenth century, thousands of people a week were taking day trips from south Wales, Bristol, Bath and Gloucester. One of the most popular excursions was the 'harvest moon special', which ran on September evenings so that people could watch the apparently distended and impossibly orange moon rising through the windows of Tintern Abbey. The spectacular, not to say Picturesque, effect of this phenomenon had been expressed a century earlier by a traveller called Charles Heath in one of the earliest guidebooks to the area, *The Excursion down the Wye from Ross to Monmouth*: 'At that part of the year,' he wrote, 'when the HEAVENS are lighted up in the fullness of their glory, by what we name the HARVEST MOON, the Abbey then presents itself in grandeur beyond the power of my abilities to express.' ('But I am having a go,' he may well have added, 'by writing certain NOUNS, for no discernible reason, in capital LETTERS.')

The most evocative description of the old railway is provided by one of the Valley's most interesting characters, Flora Klickmann. She was a writer and journalist who, from 1908 to 1931, edited *The Girl's Own Paper*, a sort of Edwardian *Cosmo Girl*. She also wrote a number of lightly fictionalised accounts of her life in the Wye Valley and how she found peace here after the bustle and stress of London, where she also had a house. These became known collectively as the 'Flower Patch' books because their titles – such as *The Flower Patch Among the Hills* and *Flower-Patch Neighbours* – always incorporated those words.

Klickmann lived in Brockweir, half a mile north of Tintern station and accessible from the A466 via a narrow cast-iron bridge over the Wye. She died there in 1958, and is buried there. It's hard to imagine anyone knowing the area better and she was much admired for her ability to recreate the simplicity of life in the Wye Valley – 'the valley of peace', as she called it – from descriptions of the smoky but nonetheless quaint train running through it, to the swirling and noisy river and its unthreatening wildlife passing the time of day.

Hard as it is to believe now, this prosperous-looking commuter village – with its restored medieval houses, one showing the remains of Tudor stone windows – was once the kind of place you wouldn't venture into without full body armour. It was a frontier town, the highest navigable point on the river for cargo ships. Here goods were transferred to and from flat-bottomed Wye boats called trows, which could safely navigate the stretches above Brockweir. Like many places on borders or frontiers – in this case it was effectively where the open sea turned into a country stream – the village seems to have existed in a state of simmering tension, and by the early 1800s was regarded as 'a lawless place of ne'er-do-wells', according to Anne Rainsbury.

There were numerous pubs and cider houses in the

village – seven and sixteen are two different numbers cited, but who knows what counted as a boozer in those days? Possibly just a couple of chairs in a living room. All of which gave the stevedores, bargemen, visiting sailors and local workmen plenty of scope for drinking, betting on cock fights and sticking one on each other. Neither did they have to waste valuable brawling time in attending Sunday service, for Brockweir was unusual in having no church – as one commentator put it, it was 'a village destitute of religious advantage'.

This was to change at the beginning of the 1830s with the arrival of missionaries from the Moravian church, which originated in what is now the Czech Republic but had an established congregation in Bristol. Amazingly, they weren't run out of town and with a nice sense of irony they built their church (in 1833) on top of a cock-fighting pit.

To reach the church, you take the footpath next to the pub car park – there's only one pub these days, the Brockweir Country Inn – and follow the eponymous weir, where gunnera the size of pub umbrellas grow, to the simple whitewashed building on the riverbank. The Moravians seem to be an unusually friendly denomination. The church door will almost certainly be open and in the vestibule will be a tray of water and squash with an invitation to 'Please help yourself to a (free) drink' and a notice of welcome: 'Our white church by the river Wye often acts as a beacon to walkers and visitors . . .'

Refreshed and back on the A466 heading north, the tree

anopy and ground vegetation are so thick and all-
encompassing in summer that you can feel as if you are
driving into a green eye socket, for which our pistachio
Mark I is ideally camouflaged. There are frequent signs
warning of falling boulders and the steeply wooded
hillside to the left is fenced off at certain points to prevent
landslips. Below the level of the road to your right, and
often invisible until you are right next to it, the river has
a mysterious antilinear topography, such that you are
often unsure which bank you are looking at: east or west,
Gloucestershire or Monmouthshire.

William Gilpin banged on at length – and not always
entirely coherently – about how the river banks, or 'side-
screens' as he called them, provide contrast and perspective, constantly revealing fresh views, like moving stage
sets, for the boat-bound tourist. His revolutionary pocket-
book, *Observations on the River Wye*, containing these
aperçus was designed specifically to be taken on a boat
trip down the river, for only from the level of the river
itself could you enjoy the full effect of the unfolding
scenery as he describes it. The boat tours had originally
lasted two days, but, after Gilpin had had his day, the
road and the railway enabled tourists to cover the
highlights of the Wye in a single day, and the tourist boats
gradually fell out of favour.

By 1896, the Ward Lock guide to *The Valley of the Wye*
is divided into two sections: 'By River' and 'By Road and
Rail'. The last commercial boat service finished in 1912
and since then the river has silted up and is too shallow

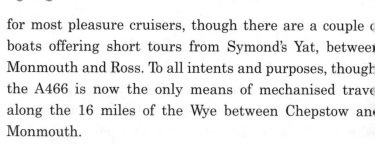

for most pleasure cruisers, though there are a couple of boats offering short tours from Symond's Yat, between Monmouth and Ross. To all intents and purposes, though, the A466 is now the only means of mechanised travel along the 16 miles of the Wye between Chepstow and Monmouth.

'Llandogo welcomes careful drivers' says the sign announcing the next village up from Brockweir. In the 1950s the sign may additionally have advised, 'Play in progress', for the A466 through Llandogo, which curves in sympathy with the outward loop of the river, was where the young Ruth Brown played tennis, so infrequent were the cars passing through.

Ruth is married to Roger Brown and together they run the village shop, called Brown's General Stores. The shop has been in the family since Roger's father opened it in 1929 and for many years it competed for trade with two other shops.

'Everyone bought locally,' says Roger, a small, dapper man now in his seventies. 'We had our milk from the local farms, eggs, butter . . .' Few people owned a car – hence Ruth's tennis work-outs in the road – so villagers confined their visits to the nearest town, Monmouth, to a Friday when the 'shoppers' bus' ran and otherwise shopped in Llandogo. Now Brown's is the only shop left in the village and people do the bulk of their shopping in Monmouth or Chepstow. But Brown's continues to serve a demand that the big supermarkets can't supply. 'Strangely enough, now everyone is going back to the way we were after the war,' explains Roger. 'We've got local farms producing sausages and bacon, we have local produce – strawberries, asparagus – and it's what people want.'

He recalls that in the 1950s the local farmer would risk runny pockets by walking round with a few eggs in them in case anyone wanted to make an impulse buy, and the petrol pump attendant would smoke whilst filling you up. Tourists generally arrived in coaches, and Roger's father opened a tearoom to serve them cream teas and Wye salmon. But, whilst happy to reminisce, Roger refuses to succumb to nostalgia for the old days. 'Everybody's better off now,' he says. 'There was poverty then. It was hard, it was very hard.'

This riverside hamlet, with its 'general stores' and b&bs, was once a centre for shipbuilding. In particular, it was the home of the trow, a flat-bottomed cargo ship designed to sail on the Lower Wye and the Severn. A sketch of the riverbank at Llandogo in 1797, owned by Chepstow Museum, shows a tourist boat in the foreground and two trows behind it. Their white sails, which stood out against the green of the wooded hillsides, were 'very picturesque', said Gilpin.

The association between the village and boats is marked by the name of a pub in the village, the Sloop Inn, while the name of another pub, near the docks in Bristol, immortalises the relationship between Llandogo and the singular vessel that used to be made here. The pub is called the Llandoger Trow, an imposing half-timbered medieval building that looks as if it holds secrets. Two

stories in particular have gained currency over the years
that it was where Daniel Defoe met Alexander Selkirk,
the real-life desert-island castaway who inspired
Robinson Crusoe; and that it was the model for either the
Admiral Benbow or the Spyglass, the two inns that
feature in *Treasure Island* by Robert Louis Stevenson.
There seems no evidence for these assertions, but
excitable tourist guides – and websites – have kept the
stories going. And the tourists lap it up and don't want to
believe that it's not true.

The Lower Wye Valley is such a bucolic spot that it's
easy to forget its proximity to and close relationship with
the sea. But in August 1802 the Wye's maritime connections were marked in the most dramatic and accidental
way when Admiral Lord Nelson, fresh from whipping the
French at the Battle of the Nile, and the Danes and
Norwegians at the Battle of Copenhagen (the one at
which he put the telescope to his blind eye), decided to
fold up his spyglass and take a private pootle down the
Wye.

It was, reckons Nelson's great-great-great grand-
daughter, Anna Tribe, who lives locally, the only holiday
he ever took – and it probably put him off taking time out
for good. Anna gives talks about her famous ancestor at
the Nelson Museum in Monmouth, which houses one of
the world's most comprehensive collections of memorabilia relating to the great man.

Nelson had hoped – and expected – not to be recognised
and expressed surprise 'at being known on such a little

gut of a river'. But as word got round that the 'hero of the Nile' and all-round greatest living Englishman was in the neighbourhood, his trip down the Wye turned into a triumphal procession. 'When they got to Monmouth, the townsfolk insisted on pulling his boat in and singing, "Hail, the conquering hero",' says Anna, who reckons that if it wasn't for her great-great-great grandfather we might all be speaking French now. Going with the flow, Nelson accepted an invitation to return to Monmouth a month later to soak up the adulation in a humble way.

He was entertained on top of a hill called the Kymin, high above the junction between the A466 and the A4136, which takes you away from the mazy Wye and into the shadowy and mysterious Forest of Dean. The Kymin, now owned by the National Trust, is notable for its Georgian Round House, a circular banqueting tower where Nelson was feted, and its Naval Temple, built following Nelson's victory on the Nile 'to perpetuate the names of those noble admirals who distinguished themselves by their glorious victories for England in the last and present wars' – which makes them sound a little like Davis Cup tennis players. Jan Morris, the celebrated Welsh travel writer, has likened the Kymin to Ootacamund, known as Snooty Ooty, a British hill-station in India at the time of the Raj where the upper classes retreated from the hoi polloi. 'Far far away is the jabber of natives!' Morris wrote of the Kymin.

The Round House, built by Monmouth bigwigs in the 1790s, was equipped with telescopes to take in the

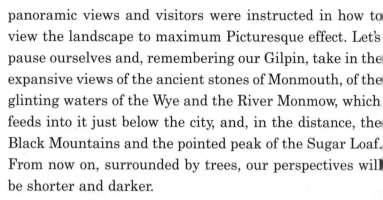

panoramic views and visitors were instructed in how to view the landscape to maximum Picturesque effect. Let's pause ourselves and, remembering our Gilpin, take in the expansive views of the ancient stones of Monmouth, of the glinting waters of the Wye and the River Monmow, which feeds into it just below the city, and, in the distance, the Black Mountains and the pointed peak of the Sugar Loaf. From now on, surrounded by trees, our perspectives will be shorter and darker.

The A4136 that takes us towards the Forest of Dean is a bit of a teaser. Within two miles of its junction with the A466 on the outskirts of Monmouth, it turns east and climbs towards the Forest. There are even triangular signs warning of deer and sheep and promising leafy wilderness, but as the road continues to run north-east, the Forest remains as a blur of trees, a brooding presence to your right-hand side.

The area known as the Forest of Dean is a raised bowl of rock that, back in the mists of pre-history, would have been vast swamp – the coal that underlies it is layers of compressed trees – and it is this geological quirk that gives the area a fortress feel. You have to climb the lip of the bowl before you can get inside it, but the A4136 merely, and frustratingly, skims along the edge of that lip.

Finally, at Mitcheldean, we take the plunge, pointing the Cambridge down the unclassified road signposted 'Westbury' that turns off the A4136 in the centre of the village. Skimming between tall hedges you can't see much at first – just a glimpse of forested hillside – but there is a palpable sense of descent into another world. The land-scape looks less tamed than much of England, though, as is usually the case with apparently pristine wilderness, man has had a considerable hand in shaping what we see.

For hundreds of years, trees were felled to produce charcoal for iron forges and oak for naval ships, and until the early twentieth century the rich green meadows and thickets of broadleaf and coniferous forest were criss-crossed with tramroads along which horses would pull wagons loaded with coal, stone and timber to the docks on the Severn and the Wye. In 1938 it became the first National Forest Park in England and is now managed by the Forestry Commission.

Just beyond Flaxley Church, built in contrasting red and grey stone, we take the right-hand turn signposted 'Littledean', which brings us out on the A4151 and into the village deep in the Forest that is the home of a 'sheep badger' called Mick Holder.

Mick's farmhouse is built on a ridge overlooking the Severn estuary. Through his living-room window he points east, across the top of the snaking river with its glistening mudbanks, to indicate the distant Cotswold hills, and the Malverns to the north. His home is like those twin theatrical masks depicting tragedy and comedy, for the other side faces dark forest – 28,000 acres of woodland, abandoned tunnels and arcane laws where Mick and his lifelong friend Henry Mills perpetuate the ancient activity of sheep badgering.

Mick is immediately reassuring on what this actually

entails: 'To badger or to badge means to agitate or to keep on the move,' he explains. 'Back in the days when nearly every household in the Forest had a few sheep, there was a saying: "Never let the sheep hear the church bells twice" – which meant they were never grazing on one spot for too long.'

The right to own sheep, and to let them roam free within the boundaries of the Forest, including the sides of roads, was bestowed on the people of the Forest of Dean by royal charter in Norman times – when mountain bikes, pet dogs and garden flowers were unlikely to come into direct confrontation with the Forest's freewheeling ovine ruminants. Now there are about 30 active 'graziers', between them 'running' about 2,000 sheep, who roam casually along roadsides and among houses – but not everyone is happy to share living space with these peaceable, if incontinent, creatures.

Mick and Henry, who are in their seventies, regard the stand-off as a conflict between old and new. As they see it, cars that park on grass verges to avoid paying car-parking fees, dogs let off the lead and careering, helmeted cyclists on weekends from the city are all hazards to their sheep, but they feel aggrieved that some people see the problem the other way round. They complain that the sheep foul footpaths, eat gardens and are a danger to traffic. 'The people who are in charge of the "progress" of our area don't want grazing sheep,' says Mick. 'They apply modern legislation and they don't even know where we are and what we are. And it's not always applicable.

192

We now have a sheep badger with an Asbo. We thought Asbos were designed as a restriction on a criminal, not to interfere with a way of life.'

Mick and Henry are torch-holders for an age whose ways and principles were forgotten long ago by the rest of England. And they feel angry and puzzled that they are being left behind in a mindless, safety-helmeted rush.

In the 1950s, says Mick, the Forest of Dean was a hive of industry. 'We had a railway station at Cinderford,' says Mick. 'Goods and passengers. RA Lister engineers had a factory there. Iron ore coming in and parts going out. A biscuit factory. A plastics manufacturer. The pits were open. Every corner shop was busy. People used to sell things out of a lean-to on the side of their houses. All gone.'

'In Blakeney,' says Henry, 'there were thirty-two shops.' He reels off the names of just the many shoe shops. 'Now there's two left.'

'Everybody had a pig,' continues Mick.

'Generally two,' adds Henry. 'Come October one'd go to the bacon factory, the other'd be hanging up in your kitchen.'

'And once you've tasted bacon that's been reared on acorn and bracken, you'll never want to buy anything else,' says Mick.

Henry, who wears his flat cap indoors, followed the rest of his family down the pit, working as a miner at Norchard Colliery, a deep coal mine on the edge of the Forest. Away from the pit, he ran sheep and fished the Severn – 'and I never took me trousers off for a week'.

Then, on 1 January 1962, he was trapped by a fall of rock. 'A slab came out and wallop! I was thirty-two then.' The near-fatal accident saved his life by cutting short his mining career – many of his relatives and friends who worked underground died prematurely from pneumoconiosis, the lung disease caused by inhaling coal dust.

He and Mick chunter and banter on, in rural burrs that sound more nineteenth century than twenty-first, about how the local bobby could call the youth to order just by issuing a warning cough, and even the violence was more wholesome. No knives – boys would fight bare-knuckle. Henry recalls two lads biffing each other for an hour, till their faces 'looked like liver'.

But radical change was just around the corner, in the next decade in fact. The railways shrank, heavy industry declined and disappeared, the population became more mobile and transient and society more centralised. By the end of the twentieth century the biggest threat to the continuation of sheep badgering in the Forest was not health-and-safety zealots or townies who didn't understand rural ways. It was an event that took place in 1988 – the closure of the maternity unit at Dilke Memorial Hospital in Cinderford, the only one in the area.

Since it closed, local babies – except the few who have had a home birth – have technically been born outside the Forest, which means they are disqualified from becoming sheep badgers, as the ancient right stipulates that you must have been born within the 'Hundred of St Briavels'.

– roughly speaking, the area now called the Forest of Dean. Though a few babies every year continue to be born within the Forest – whether by accident or design – and a few young lads are showing an interest in being a leader of the flock and having stand-offs with picnickers and boy-racers, Henry and Mick are pessimistic. 'The next fifty or sixty years, I shudder to think the way things will be,' says Mick.

Back in the Austin and slowing down for the sheep – after all, they may be Mick's or Henry's – we proceed on the A4151 through the village of Littledean and take the unclassified road on the left for Upper and Lower Soudley, and from there wind down to Blakeney. We turn right on to the A48 and after half a mile right again, following the 'Scenic route' signs that take us back into the heart of the Forest, through hamlets of sandstone cottages with names such as Tump and Orchard, over rushing streams and past red telephone boxes.

Another right turn in the middle of the Forest takes us to Speech House, a seventeenth-century former royal hunting lodge that also served as the local parliament, or Verderers' Court, and is now a hotel. Here we turn left on the B4226 and presently, on the right-hand side, reach Hopewell Colliery, the home of another endangered species: the freeminer.

Freeminers are so-called because, like sheep badgers, they enjoy a privilege granted them by ancient royal charter: the freedom to mine for coal (and iron ore, ochre and stone) anywhere in the Forest. To qualify as a freeminer you have to have been born within the Hundred of St Briavels, be over 21 and to have worked at least a year and a day in a mine within the Hundred. Oh, and you have to be a man.

Hopewell Colliery – whose landscaped workings are, inevitably, grazed by sheep – is an old coal mine with sloping shafts that run for hundreds of feet into the side of a hill. It is now a museum where two freeminers, Robin Morgan and Richard Daniels, conduct guided tours of the old workings, telling stories of hardship, disease and camaraderie, of the deadly 'black damp' – a mixture of nitrogen and carbon dioxide that gathers in badly ventilated workings – and pointing out sections of fossilised tree in the roof rock and an otter's paw print by the side of an underground stream.

The commercial extraction of coal in the Forest of Dean – though it continues on a very small scale – is little known about now. We associate coal with the industrial heartlands of south Wales and south Yorkshire, not rural backwaters, but in the 1940s and 1950s there were 10,000 miners working here.

Robin Morgan, an astonishingly fit and lithe 73, remembers when six deep mines were open and over 1,000 men worked in a single pit. 'All the mining was done exactly as it was hundreds of years ago except we had cutting machines and conveyor belts.' The large collieries had all closed by 1965 and since then individuals or small teams of freeminers have continued to work the coalfaces. Now there are thought to be about

150 freeminers left, of whom about 30 regularly attend meetings and about a dozen actually work the coal.

When Robin opened Hopewell as a museum in 1997 he gave up the mining, but now – partly out of economic necessity and partly, you suspect, because it is in his blood – he has opened up a working shaft at Hopewell ('She'll make a few bob,' he says matter-of-factly) and become a miner again. Well into his eightieth decade – an age when for many the day's most strenuous activity is buying the paper at the corner shop – he is enduring again the kind of physical hardship and difficult and potentially dangerous working conditions that would defeat most men a third his age. And unlike the sheep badgers, and notwithstanding the closure of that maternity unit, he sees a future for freeminers in the Forest of Dean. 'I think the time will come when the pits will come back,' he says. 'There is a lot of coal here and it will be got because it's needed.'

The Forest is a self-contained place, and you enter and leave it suddenly. The playwright Dennis Potter, whose dark and groundbreaking dramas drew on his childhood here, described it as 'a heart-shaped place between two rivers [the Wye and the Severn], somehow slightly cut off from them'. The map shows that 'heart-shaped' is accurate. But it is not a stylised, St Valentine's heart, more the knobbly, asymmetrical shape of our principal vital organ – gritty and functional as well as beautiful.

The Forest also feels decidedly cut off. From Hopewell we continue west on the B4226 and within five minutes of leaving the old colliery, the Forest of Dean is no longer visible in the rearview mirror – one imagines the trees, in a Potteresque moment (Harry as well as Dennis), discreetly closing their canopies like a drawbridge behind us. A right turn takes the Cambridge onto the B4432 on the outskirts of Coleford, and this crosses the A4136 and continues north for two miles to the fluttering Union flag that marks the Wye's most famous beauty spot.

Symond's Yat Rock is a craggy limestone prow jutting some 500 feet above the Wye Valley, upon which you stand like an explorer scanning new lands. The view from the Rock is a cliché in the sense that it has been much photographed and painted, but it is still endlessly fascinating and beautiful, mainly because the Wye decides to confound us with its contortions at this point, squiggling around like a Rococo flourish with a quill pen. To the north it bulges in a loop round a floodplain, to the east the wooded gorge plunges dizzily beneath one's feet, and to the west its far bank seems to be straining to create a pinch-point of this prow of land on which we stand. Which is upstream and which down? Which Herefordshire and which Gloucestershire?

Into this topographical conundrum Barbara Britton was born in 1940. By then her mother, Dorothy Jones, had been the local subpostmistress for six years. 'The small black and white bungalow was the old post office and it's where I was born,' she says (it remains in the family, as Barbara's son now lives in it). Dorothy ran it as a 'non telegraph and non money-order office' for more than 55 years, till her retirement in May 1995 (her first and only burglary occurred in 1994). Barbara has vivid memories of the 1950s, when coach companies brought daytrippers from all over the country: Baynham's from Ross-on-Wye, Black and White from Cheltenham, Wessex from Bristol and Byngs of Southsea. 'You'd have coaches parked outside the post office and snaking all down the road,' she recalls. 'Everyone wanted a postcard and a stamp. It wasn't an open-door policy. If they wanted service they had to ring a bell, so you were constantly being interrupted.'

Barbara's father, Wilf Jones, worked part time as a ferryman between Symond's Yat East and Symond's Yat West. These riverside hamlets, facing each other across the Wye, are linked, as they have been for many years, by two 'rope' ferries, one from the Ferrie Inn on the west side, the other from the Saracen's Head on the east. The ferryman literally hauls the boat across by means of a rope tied between the riverbanks. In 1942, when the river was in flood, the rope snapped while Wilf was taking four passengers across to the western side, but he managed to save them from drowning in what the *Ross Gazette* described as 'a miraculous escape' due to 'the magnificent work of a ferryman'.

In 1947 young Barbara had her own extraordinary experience on the river. There had been heavy snowfalls. 'It was so deep everywhere was cut off and when the snow melted the river was in flood,' she says. When her mother rowed her across the river, they floated in through the bedroom window of a friend's house on the other side.

On the surface remarkably little seems to have changed on the river in the intervening years. The ancient inns and hand-pulled ferries are still there. People still take boats to the little riverside church of St Dubricius near Symond's Yat West for weddings and funerals. But the sense of community has gone, reckons Barbara. 'There's very few of what we call the old families left now,' she says. 'I could name virtually every family in every house, but there's only half a dozen now. It's all incomers.' A trend started, you might say, by William Gilpin.

There's a supreme irony in his experience of this part of the river. When he reached Symond's Yat Rock he had been planning to go ashore to climb the rock and enjoy 'some very noble river views'. But it was raining, so the poor lamb stayed on his boat. Here, below the beetling limestone crags, the riverside woods have the mustiness and acoustics of a church interior and the water meadows are carpeted in spring by buttercups and wild mint. It is the most spectacularly Picturesque spot on the journey.

'It was a paradise really,' says Barbara.

And Gilpin, huddled in his oilskins and pontificating in his notebook, missed it.

Chapter 6

The Trossachs

Callander – A84 to Kilmahog – A821 through Brig o'
Turk to Loch Katrine – Duke's Pass to Aberfoyle
– B829 to Loch Arklet – unclassified road to
Stronachlachar – unclassified road to Inversnaid

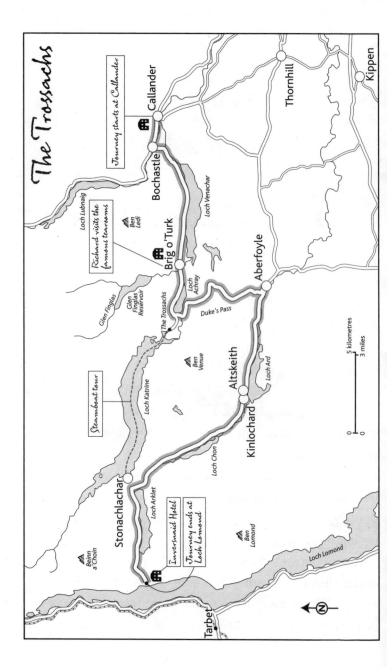

The Trossachs

Journey starts at Callander

Richard visits the famous tearooms

Steamboat tour

Inversnaid Hotel

Journey ends at Loch Lomond

Loch Lubnaig

Ben Ledi

Callander

Bochastle

Thornhill

Kippen

Brig o'Turk

Loch Venachar

Aberfoyle

Glen Finglas

Glen Finglas Reservoir

Loch Achray

Duke's Pass

The Trossachs

Ben Venue

Altskeith

Loch Ard

Kinlochard

Loch Katrine

Loch Chon

Stonachlachar

Loch Arklet

Beinn a'Choin

Ben Lomond

Loch Lomond

Tarbet

N

5 kilometres
3 miles
0
0

The Trossachs

THERE IS SOMETHING PERVERSE ABOUT this: the gear stick on the Bentley Mark VI is on the right of the driver, between the padded armchair of a seat (leather supplied by Connolly, purveyor of luxury interior hide to Rolls-Royce, Jaguar and Ferrari) and the leather-and-walnut door; whereas on the left-hand drive model it is where it should be: on the central column. Think of it as royal prerogative, for this post-war, classic, top-end motor was a monarch on the roads of the 1950s, turning the democracy of affordable Fords into deferential rabbits in its headlights.

It was marketed as a 'sports saloon' – its 4.6 litre engine could reach 100mph – but has the air of a mobile don's study. The gearshift is eccentric and the clockwork indicators are like stress-relievers invented by a mad professor. You twist a vertical bar on the walnut-veneer facia – clockwise for right, anti-clockwise for left – and the silver indicator stalk pops out just behind your ear, cuckoo-clock-like, from the frame between front and back door, folding back in when the clockwork has run down. And it runs down fairly swiftly, so if the traffic lights take a while to change, or your blood pressure is rising like an overheating radiator, you might have to do it several times.

The Bentley had two sets of keys – one for one's chauffeur and another that opened the glovebox, where one fancies finding a jar of Gentleman's Relish, two pairs of half-moon spectacles, and a leather-bound copy of Herodotus 'acquired' from Balliol College library in 1932. The tray tables in the rear will do splendidly for crumpets and quince jam at four.

For the duration of our tour of The Trossachs, the Mark VI will be, aptly enough, our Monarch of the Glen. For this is quintessential romantic and rugged Scotland – and it was more or less invented in the early nineteenth century. Not the landscape, of course – the reality of these lochs and glens and heather, overlaid by swirling mists, is more dramatic and stirring than any film or fiction – but the way people have looked at and thought about that landscape has been carefully shaped.

We start in Callander, a town that lies on a geographical and cultural fault line, explore a region popularised by a Lowland Scot, Sir Walter Scott, who generated a modern notion of the Highlands, and end at a famous loch where an English poet wrote a plea for the conservation of the natural world. On the way, we pull the Bentley's long bonnet round the near one hundred bends of Scotland's most scenic road pass, then thread the old queen along single-lane lochside lanes where, impertinently, lesser vehicles occasionally force her to wait her turn in the designated passing places. The cheek of it!

Deference may have passed since the Mark VI lorded it over lesser marques, but it is still very much the order of the day in the fictional world of *Dr Finlay's Casebook*. This long-running television series, which first hit our postage-stamp-size screens on 16 August 1962, was based on a character created by the Scottish novelist A. J. Cronin. It recounted the experiences of a junior partner, played by Bill Simpson, in a country medical practice in the 1920s. The tension – never overstepping the bounds of deference – between new and old, Simpson's Dr Finlay and his senior partner, Dr Cameron (Andrew Cruickshank), drove the series on for nearly nine years in an era when TV viewing, especially in a prime Sunday slot, was a countrywide participatory experience. 'After the first three stories,' wrote Andrew Cruickshank in his autobiography, 'it was very evident that the moral tone of the series had captured the early Sunday evening audience which usually goes to church.'

Finlay and Cameron, aided by their housekeeper, Janet (Barbara Mullen), served the fictitious community of Tannochbrae. Interior scenes were shot in a studio in London (and later Glasgow), but all the location work was done in Callander, and it was Callander that became, de facto, Dr Finlay's town. 'Arden House' was the name of the doctors' residence and the prim, Presbyterian manner in which Janet answered the quaint telephonic device when a farmer's wife rang up with some unmentionable affliction was soon being aped by comics and schoolkids across the land: 'Arrden Hoose?' she would say, with a hint of suspicion and disapproval.

The series played out across a decade of immense cultural upheaval, characterised by Philip Larkin's mordant assertion that sexual intercourse was 'invented' in 1963, through peace, love and psychedelia, to the death of hippiedom in the violent anti-Vietnam War demos of 1969. And still Janet sighed and said, 'It's a wild night in the hills. I wish Dr Cameron were back.' This made the series both reassuring and ripe for being sent up. Sharp-eyed viewers noticed, for example, that the producers had solved the problem of the inside and outside of the doctors' house being several hundred miles apart by depriving the studio set of windows.

The exterior of 'Arden House' was a guesthouse high on a wooded hill behind Callander called Auchengower House. In 1968 this handsome Victorian villa dropped the quotation marks around Arden House and adopted that name in real life. Tourism and fiction are often sly bed-fellows, as we have discovered. Arden House is still a guesthouse and its bedrooms are named after characters in the series – Janet, Mistress Niven (the midwife), Drs Cameron, Finlay and Snoddie – and a black doctor's bag sits permanently on the stairs, in reference both to the series and to *Adventures of a Black Bag*, the collection of stories by A. J. Cronin that inspired it. On the wall near the bag is a signed note from Bill Simpson: 'To Arden House and all who sail in her on behalf of Janet and the "doctors".' But memories of Dr Finlay, among generations brought up on *Casualty* and *ER*, are evidently fading. 'The number of people who say, "Someone's left a bag . . .",' says one of the co-owners, William Jackson, pointing at the battered leather case on the stairs.

In 1966, when the *Casebook* series was in full swing, a real life Dr Finlay – a Dr Ian Williams – arrived in Callander to take up a post as junior partner in the town's medical practice. Dr Williams, who is now retired after a 'wonderful' career, recalls that '*Dr Finlay's Casebook* didn't have altogether a favourable response from the community.' Though the townsfolk were for the most part proud to be associated with the decent, God-fearing folk of 'Tannochbrae', the filming could be disruptive. 'The camera crews were a bit arrogant,' he says. 'Their way of life, from the south of England, was not the way of life of a Highland town.' And very little has changed in that regard in the past 40-odd years.

Medically, he says, the series was 'reasonably authentic, and there were some aspects that hadn't changed when I went there.' The routine for one. Dr Williams would start at half past nine, do three surgeries and spend the rest of the time visiting patients. 'Doing the rounds was almost a social occasion,' he says. 'You'd go in and a lady would have a tray with two glasses and a bottle of sherry on it. You'd talk, and it would be several minutes before you got down to business. It was a very good relationship and that was why I was happy.' In the evenings he might have to drive out to a farm to 'settle down' a dying patient for the night – death at home was much more common than now and had 'more dignity' to it. 'Given more time, GPs could provide the service that's now provided by old people's homes,' he says. Like Drs Finlay and Cameron, Dr Williams knew his patients as people and cared for them as friends.

'One thing I was taught [during medical training] in the 1950s was the idea that you had twenty-four-hour responsibility – total responsibility for the physical, mental, even social welfare of your patients,' he says. 'It worked both ways. You had respect for patients and they had respect for you.' It is a subject he feels passionately about and it goes to the heart of how Britain has changed in the past 50 years, or at least how many people old enough to look back across half a century believe that it has changed.

Dr Williams remembers a hierarchical community in which the police sergeant, the nurse – she was 'district nurse, midwife and health visitor' rolled into a single, no doubt well-upholstered figure – and doctor were among the most important people in town. *Heartbeat* territory once again. 'There's been a loss of respect,' he says sadly, 'but it's more than respect, it's almost affection. Patients were friends and they relied on you.'

In 1966, the year that Dr Williams arrived in Callander, it was, he recalls, a very sleepy town of a couple of thousand people: 'They still had a tailor. A very good greengrocer. A cobbler. It was pretty self-sufficient.' Forty years on, it now has a Tesco Express instead, but the haggis served in its restaurants is still authentic and Callander is still a sleepy place with an absent-minded air, strung out for two miles along the A84, as if it kept forgetting to end.

It was planned and built this way as a new town in the eighteenth century and attracted a vanguard of travellers curious to see The Trossachs – 'persons of taste who are desirous of seeing nature in her rudest and unpolished state', observed the local minister in 1794. Perhaps inevitably, these included Wordsworth and his sister Dorothy. But it was the arrival of the railway in 1858 that turned Callander into 'the gateway to The Trossachs'. And this is as good a time as any to consider what a trossach may possibly be. The first answer is that, like trousers or binoculars, trossachs are never referred to in the singular; the second is that no one knows, or is willing to let on. Strictly speaking, The Trossachs – *Na Troisichean* in Gaelic – is the term used to denote the hills between Lochs Katrine and Achray, where, wrote Sir Walter Scott in his epic poem, *The Lady of the Lake*, 'Their rocky summits, spilt and rent/ Formed turret, dome or battlement/ Or seemed fantastically set/ With cupola or minaret.' But it has come to apply further afield, to the attractive configuration of glens and lochs from Loch

Katrine to Aberfoyle. In any case, if you don't know what a trossach actually is, how can you claim to know precisely where it is to be found?

In honour of this singular landscape, the wealthy of Edinburgh and Glasgow built holiday homes – sturdy Victorian villas like Arden House – and locals moved into their back rooms in the holiday season and let out the front to paying guests, as was the way of things. As a teenager, Robert Louis Stevenson stayed in Callander in 1866, and nearly 30 years later, when the author of *Kidnapped* and *Treasure Island* was living in the South Pacific, he experienced a dramatic moment of déjà vu. He had been standing on the verandah of his house on Samoa, Vailima, when he was overcome with 'a heave of extraordinary and apparently baseless emotion. I literally staggered.' Then he realised he had been thinking of Callander: 'Highland huts, and peat smoke, and the brown swirling rivers, and wet clothes, and whisky, and the romance of the past.' He died the following year without seeing Scotland again.

The romance of the past certainly clings to Callander – real or ersatz. The secondhand bookshop hasn't heard of squidgy sofas, café lattes or cyber cafés, but boasts a stag's head, a stuffed owl and some violins affixed to the back wall. A poster outside the Highland Arts Studios says, 'If your name is here you have a tartan' – and proceeds to list the contents of the phonebook, from Abbot to Wylie. And in Wallace News they sell old-fashioned sweets in jars: pan drops, Clyde tofymints (sic), mixed oddfellows, sour plooms, liquorice satins, Berwick cockles and kola kubes.

But the ace up Callander's tartan sleeve is the hairy hero himself, Rob Roy, after whom its visitor centre is named ('Meet Rob Roy MacGregor at the Gateway to his Beautiful Homelands'). This seems a trifle disingenuous, seeing as the town didn't actually exist in the early eighteenth century when the Highland outlaw Robert MacGregor was making a monkey of English landowners and their Lowland Scots lackeys. He was born on the shore of Loch Katrine, to the west, and died at Balquhidder. But Callander is just playing the tourist game here. It is now the 'gateway' to a notional place called 'Rob Roy Country', and our Monarch of the Glen is about to proceed there in sedate and regal fashion.

But first let's glance at a map – there's an old cloth-bound Ordnance Survey job in the glovebox, if you have the key – where we see that Callander lies near a natural border that runs roughly south–west to north–east: to the north, rugged hills; to the south, Lowland pastures. This is the Highland Boundary Line, a geological hair-fracture that marks the precise point at which the Lowlands stop and the Highlands start. But its significance is not confined to geology.

Highlands and Lowlands denote two entirely different ways of living, thinking and behaving. The clash between the two goes to the heart of the Rob Roy legend. The old Highland way, as embodied by Rob Roy, was martial and rebellious, based on courage and honour. Highlanders lived in clans, or tribes, in inhospitable and inaccessible mountain terrain, spoke Gaelic, had lots of facial hair, ran after their food and shot it, and rustled cattle for a living, their lands of heather and rock being no good for farming. The Lowlanders, and their English landlords, cultivated the land, believed in law and order, feared God, honoured the king, and bought their food in Tesco. The old and the new – and we know which order prevailed. And now the forces of tourism package the old in romantic colours and sell it to the new. Clever, that.

Our route steers a literal and metaphorical line between rock and pasture, past and present, as we leave Callander on the A84 through a tree-lined avenue and drive towards the bulk of Ben Ledi, its summit rising to nearly 3,000 feet. To the left are water meadows, to the right steep wooded hillsides. The divide couldn't be clearer.

At Kilmahog we turn left on to the A821, crossing the River Teith on an old stone bridge. On the left is the welcoming-looking Lade Inn and we are just noting the roadsign that says 'The Trossachs Trail', and wondering whether it is too early for a snifter, when a logging truck thunders by – a reminder that this 'wild' landscape is managed and shaped by man.

By far the biggest landowner in the Loch Lomond and The Trossachs National Park is Forestry Commission Scotland and they have blanketed the hillsides in non-native conifers – mainly the fast-growing sitka spruce. Just 15 per cent of woodland is broadleaf, but there are plans to plant more birch and oak as the conifers reach maturity and are felled. This landscape – the monoculture of dark green trees, the jagged horizons formed by their conical tops – has been transformed from the days of Rob Roy when the high hills of the Trossachs would have been heather-clad moorland.

On a rolling, winding road we drop down towards Loch Venachar, on which a cluster of white sails stands out against the dark green forestry plantations on the loch's southern shore. There is bracken growing alongside the road, sheep grazing on the foreshore and mist – that damnable, romantic mist through which Rob Roy and his boys were always appearing and disappearing – enveloping the hills in front.

Now the road hits the shoreline, so we are driving almost level with the loch for a mile or so, before climbing back inland and reaching the romantically named village of Brig o' Turk. What does it mean? 'Bridge of the wild boar,' says James Lindsay, who owns the Brig o' Turk Tea Room on the right-hand side. 'Back in the 1300s when Scotland had kings and queens this was their hunting ground.'

Dr Ian Williams, the real-life Dr Finlay, isn't convinced by this explanation. So let's call a truce and put Brig o' Turk in the same etymological drawer as Trossachs so we can stop wondering what it means. The important thing about this hamlet, in any case, is that it has a tearoom, which caters for both tourists and villagers. 'The locals support it greatly,' says James. 'They come in and get lathered on a Friday night.'

The quaint and unusual nature of this institution has lent Brig o' Turk global renown. 'If anybody anywhere in the world knows Brig o' Turk, they know it from the tearoom,' says James Lindsay. 'I was in the middle of the Nullarbor Plain in Australia and this guy said, "Brig o' Turk? Isn't that the place with the green hut?"' The tearoom is indeed a green hut, made of wood and dating back to 1923, when it was built specifically as a place to take tea and scones and not, as people suppose, something else. 'People say that it was a village hall or a post office or, bizarrely, a cricket pavilion,' says Lindsay, a Glaswegian who went native here a long time ago and is proud of the history, fame and eccentricity of his tearoom.

On a wall hangs a photograph taken in 1922 of the spot where the tearoom was built the following year. The hardstanding is already in place and in the background, looking curious, is a cow. James says that an old lady still living in Brig o' Turk remembers the name of that cow, but not the name of the person who owned it. 'The tearoom was built – you won't believe this – by a direct descendant of Rob Roy MacGregor,' says James. 'His niece still lives in the village.' All this is apparently true: tartan tripe is not on the menu of the Brig o' Turk Tea Room.

Other photographs on its walls mark the tearoom's high point of fame, when it appeared in the 1959 film *The 39 Steps*, a remake of the Alfred Hitchcock movie of 1935, which was itself adapted, pretty loosely, from the John Buchan thriller of that name. The film starred Kenneth More, the quintessential English screen actor of the

1950s. Three years earlier, he had starred in that most stirringly patriotic of all English films, *Reach for the Sky*, the biopic of the Second World War fighter ace Douglas Bader, who lost his legs but continued flying, undeterred. In it More had captured to perfection Bader's stiff upper lip and quiet heroism, and now he played another archetypally understated British hero, John Buchan's Richard Hannay.

Brig o' Turk Tea Room's big moment comes when Hannay, on the run from the police, disguises himself among a group of cyclists out for a spin. Here they come, sweeping round the corner by the tearoom, which is renamed the Gallows Café for the film; here they are, a happy, wholesome bunch, enjoying tea and chatter in the tearoom itself. 'They were the Clackmannanshire Cycle Club,' says James Lindsay. 'Occasionally, the sons and daughters of people in the film come out here and make themselves known as their offspring.' The use of a cycling club in the film simply reflected the popularity of cycling in the 1950s, and the A821 through Brig o' Turk was a hugely popular route, among both cyclists and motorcyclists, at a time when there were far fewer cars on the road. 'Older folk remember that it was just like the film,' says Lindsay. 'You'd have one car parked outside the tearoom, but fifty bicycles.'

It would have been good to be around then, he reckons: 'It was pre-Forestry Commission days and the scenery would've been brilliant.' Even in the 1960s, when he first came here, he remembers the landscape being more open.

'The good thing is that the Forestry Commission is not going to do any more of that blanket planting. They're more conscientious and are using more native species. You see bits of rock formations and undulations that you could never see before. It's only recently that people have been able to see Loch Achray [a mile west of Brig o' Turk]. It's a change for the better.'

A newspaper cutting on the wall celebrates another momentous event in the history of Brig o' Turk, when it was hit by an earthquake measuring just under three on the Richter Scale in 2003. 'It shook all the soot down the chimneys,' recalls Lindsay. The village lies on the Highland boundary fault and there is a history of vertical and sideways movements.

An earlier earthquake – involving plenty of movement, both literal and metaphorical, in a variety of directions – had occurred at Brig o' Turk in 1853, when the art critic John Ruskin, his wife Effie and the portrait painter John Everett Millais came to stay in a cottage here. They too were on The Trossachs trail, and Ruskin wanted his friend Millais to paint his portrait. The resulting famous painting, showing Ruskin, hat in hand, standing by a waterfall in Glen Finglas (immediately north of the village), is not the only lasting outcome of this holiday *à trois*. When they arrived, Millais hero-worshipped Ruskin. By the time they left, Ruskin was getting on his nerves, as was the continuing bad weather. 'The dreariness of mountainous country in wet weather is beyond everything,' he wrote to his fellow artist Holman Hunt.

But his biggest dilemma was that he had developed a passion for Effie. And Effie – still a virgin after several years of marriage because Ruskin had issues with the female body – was partial to Millais. When she left Ruskin the following year – filing for annulment on the grounds of non-consummation – and later married Millais, it was one of the greatest scandals of the Victorian era.

Leaving a trio of Victorian bosoms seething with repressed passion and frustration, we continue over the Brig o' Turk itself, a stone bridge with low walls that crosses the burn tumbling down from Glen Finglas, and reach the shores of Loch Achray. Near the far end of the loch, on the left-hand side of the road and sited on the foreshore, is Trossachs Church, with an external bell in its open arch tower and three diagonal bands of tiles decorating the roof.

Millais, perhaps needing to let off steam by this stage, got the giggles when he attended a service here. The bow-legged 'precentor' had a wheezy voice and his shaggy terrier, 'the image of his master', joined in the singing, assisted by a few collies'.

In the graveyard alongside the loch there is a head-stone to William Lochied Cameron Graham 'who died on July 14th 1915 as the result of an accident while on duty aboard the hospital ship Madras in Bombay Harbour', and another commemorating the sacrifice of three brothers Macpherson, killed on the Western Front. Inside the church a monument lists the names of all the native sons who died in the First World War – 18, from population of just 300.

To look in the rearview mirror for a moment, this statistic makes more likely one of the apparently whimsical explanations for the arboreal freak known as the Bicycle Tree, a couple of miles back in Brig o'Turk village. This old sycamore, a quarter-mile north of the tearoom on the left-hand side of the Glen Finglas road, is called the Bicycle Tree because it sprouts from its trunk bits of rusty old bike. 'There's various stories about how the bike got there,' says James Lindsay. 'One is that some geezer left it there to go to the First World War and never came back.' And the tree, like a comforting arm, grew round it.

The A821 continues past the 'candlesnuffer' towers of the old Trossachs Hotel, now a timeshare complex with lawns manicured to the perfection of a golf fairway in St Andrews. When J. M. Barrie, the creator of Peter Pan, stayed at the hotel in 1917, he wrote to a friend, 'It is preeminently the spot where you are supposed to stand on a rock and recite Sir Walter Scott from the guidebook.' They all came, you see – the Victorian and Edwardian chattering classes – to see The Trossachs and visit the places immortalised in *The Lady of the Lake*. But they had to pretend they were doing it in an ironic way, like intellectuals who buy Abba CDs and watch reality TV.

We, however, will proceed in entirely unironic fashion on the A821 to the western end of Loch Achray, where the road takes a sharp left to Aberfoyle. We shall go this way presently, but for now, and watching out for coaches on the tight bends, we go straight on, winding for a mile along the side of a wooded valley before dropping to the head of Loch Katrine – and deep into the world of Sir Walter Scott. Trossachs Pier, at this eastern end of the loch, is where tourists once flocked to enter the topography of *The Lady of the Lake.*

Scott, born in Edinburgh to a Borders family, had a romanticised, Lowland view of the Highlands. After writing epic poetry, he churned out historical novels such as *Waverley*, *Ivanhoe* and, of course, *Rob Roy*, all of which reflected his establishment sympathies. *The Lady of the Lake* was published in May 1810 and utilised real locations to tell the story of Ellen Douglas, exiled on an island in Loch Katrine, and her three suitors.

The context is the historic conflict between the crown and the clans. The poem starts with a stag hunt that takes us, via the route of the A821, to the shores of Lake Katrine (don't worry; the stag gets away) and ends happily, if predictably, with the clan chieftain biting the heather and Ellen getting her man (not without a twist – the mysterious knight proves to be a very special person indeed . . .). *The Lady of the Lake* is full of high-flown description of real places: '. . . gleaming with the setting sun/ One burnish'd sheet of living gold/ Loch-Katrine lay beneath him rolled/ In all her length far winding lay/ With promontory, creek and bay/ And islands that, empurpled bright/ Floated amid the livelier light.' And just in case we don't get it, Scott provides exhaustive notes explaining precise locations.

With its archaic language and tum-ti-tum rhythms – not to mention the fact that it takes hours to get through – *The Lady of the Lake* has been deeply unfashionable and little read in recent years (though is said to be making a comeback in Scottish schools). But its combination of the ephemeral and the real captured the imagination of late Georgian society. The poem sold in bucketloads and – in a forerunner of the Captain Corelli effect – readers flocked to see Loch Katrine, Ellen's Isle at its eastern end and Brig o' Turk.

Scott, in his compulsion to turn The Trossachs into a theme park, didn't stop there. In 1817 he published the novel *Rob Roy*, which romanticised the exploits of the 'Highland Robin Hood' and Jacobite sympathiser Robert MacGregor a century earlier. And in 1822 he organised a propaganda visit to Scotland by George IV, the first time the reigning monarch had been to Scotland since 1650. Scott persuaded the king it would be a gesture of conciliation if he were to wear the traditional Highland garb of tartan and a kilt, and the king had the bright idea of adding pink tights to the mix. The result – much lampooned at the time – nevertheless helped cement a new sense of Scottish identity and one that tourism has exploited more or less ever since. Admittedly, the pink tights never caught on, but images of tartan, kilts, Rob Roy and swirling mist still create a composite picture of Scotland in the minds of visitors.

Nowadays, the thousands of people who still flock here probably associate Sir Walter Scott more with the steamer of that name that services Loch Katrine than with the author who set the ball rolling. But there's something appropriate about the modern-day *Sir Walter* continuing the work of its progenitor as it ferries people from site to site along the loch, like an elderly, pipe-smoking gent giving a proud tour of his flower beds.

With its white hull, wooden wheelhouse and cream-painted, slanting funnel, the steam ship *Sir Walter Scott* has a drowsy air of Edwardian summers. The hooter blows, the telegraph rings and we slip from the jetty, presently reaching our cruising speed of eight knots. The steamer is 110 feet long, but the sheer scale of the landscape dwarfs her: from the summits of the peaks that loom to the south and north of the loch's eastern end, Ben Venue and Ben An, she looks like an insect, a water-boatman poised on the skin of the loch. But we are safely aboard and looking from a different perspective. Beneath her stripy awnings it's possible to watch Ellen's Isle slip by the starboard side while enjoying our Loch Katrine or Rob Roy specials from the bar – that's a coffee 'with a wee dram' or a hot chocolate with a dash of brandy, respectively – while the captain burbles on with his commentary. He may tell you, for instance, that as Loch Katrine is fed by many small burns, its waters are particularly clean and healthy – which is why the loch has been supplying Glasgow, 35 miles south, with drinking water since 1859.

Before then, the city was insanitary and rife with disease. Water was sold from barrels or taken from

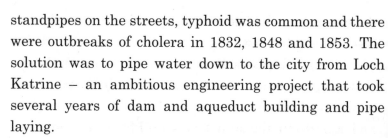

standpipes on the streets, typhoid was common and there were outbreaks of cholera in 1832, 1848 and 1853. The solution was to pipe water down to the city from Loch Katrine – an ambitious engineering project that took several years of dam and aqueduct building and pipe laying.

One effect of turning the loch into a reservoir was that the water level was artificially raised – the 'far-projecting precipice' mentioned in *The Lady of the Lake*, Granchach Rock, is now largely underwater. On 14 October 1859 the Loch Katrine Water Supply Scheme was officially opened by Queen Victoria, who sailed up Loch Katrine in *Sir Walter*'s predecessor, *Rob Roy*. She turned a tap, and half an hour later sparkling loch water flowed into the Gorbals, where it was greeted with much suspicious sniffing – and disinfected with whisky just in case. The practice has continued to this day.

The SS *Sir Walter Scott* is a Loch Katrine institution, for she has been here since 1899. But she arrived with the tourists, along a once well-worn route. The steamer was built in Dumbarton in sections and these were sailed up Loch Lomond to Inversnaid on the loch's eastern bank. From there, they were carried by horse-drawn wagon to Stronachlachar at the western end of Loch Katrine – precisely the route followed by tourists in the early part of the nineteenth century.

Almost every loch had its pleasure steamer in the nineteenth and early twentieth centuries, and the SS *Sir Walter Scott* wasn't the first on Loch Katrine. That dubious honour had gone to the paddle steamer *Gypsy* in 1843. She didn't last long – she was scuttled by the crew of the original tourist boat, an eight-oared galley called *Water Witch*, which had had a monopoly on the tourist business till *Gypsy* came along. She was never salvaged and is still on the loch bed somewhere. Two steamers called *Rob Roy* followed, between them seeing service from 1845 to 1900, and now the SS *Sir Walter Scott* is the only screw steamer surviving in passenger service in Scotland. She remains a steamer to avoid the possibility of polluting the loch with diesel and until 2007 continued to burn coal. She now burns bio-fuel and her homely aroma of coal and soot has been replaced by an agricultural whiff (steamers on Ullswater and Windermere in the Lake District converted to diesel long ago).

Leaving *Sir Walter* to sail off in a cloud of neeps and tatties, and pausing only to stock up on tartan and Celtic silverware in the Trossachs Pier gift shop, let's turn the Bentley round and retrace our route to the western end of Loch Achray. Ahead is the road we came up from Callander and Brig o' Turk. A sharp right turn takes us on to the 'Trossachs New Road', also known as the Duke's Pass, which wasn't built until the 1880s. Before then it had been a winding track across The Trossachs themselves: an extraordinary topography of bracken- and heather-covered hills – the 'turret, dome or battlement' described in *The Lady of the Lake* – with views of lochs and mountaintops unfolding all around like a series of postcards.

On the southern side lies Aberfoyle, a rival to Callander for the title of 'gateway to The Trossachs'. In 1882 it became the terminus of a branch line built to bring in tourists and the local landowner, the Duke of Montrose, decided to turn the path across The Trossachs into a carriage road connecting with the road to Loch Katrine. And this is the road we now turn into. The cream-painted mileposts hidden in the bracken of the bank – in shape, a cross between a pyramid and a mushroom – were put there in honour of Queen Victoria when she came to open the Loch Katrine Water Supply Scheme in 1859. Ahead is a Forestry Commission sign announcing 'Duke's Pass, scenic drive' – which it most certainly is. Past the Loch Achray Hotel the road is at loch level, but then it begins to climb the far shore of the loch – with views behind us of Trossachs Church on the opposite bank – between verges of heather and bracken.

Back and forth the road winds, through stands of silver birch, while the slopes of Ben Venue materialise and dematerialise through the mist to our right. The Mark VI's powerful engine is taking it steady in second gear, when we nose round a bend – and have to swerve to avoid a dark, mysterious figure standing at the side of the road. In the mist that comes swirling down from Ben Venue, it could, for a split second, be an apparition from the pages of Scott. And certainly the identity of this figure must be guarded as closely as that of 'James Fitz-James' in *The Lady of the Lake*. All we need to know is that it stands knee-high to a Harley-Davidson, it is presently encased in motorcycle leathers and helmet, and it blogs by the codename of 'Gorgeous Biker Chick'.

GBC is that rare thing, a woman who is crazy about vintage motorcycles – re-building them, repairing them, riding them and writing about them. She contributes to a classic bike magazine, is Secretary of both the Grampian Classic Motorcycle Club and the North-East Scottish section of the Vintage Motorcycle Club, and is riding her bike to every county in Scotland to raise money for charity. And whenever she can, she rides her favourite stretch of road, the Duke's Pass between Loch Achray and Aberfoyle. Her mission is to promote the riding of old bikes – 'They're not just meant to be polished, they're meant to be ridden' – and presently she is bent over the frame of her 1962 200cc Triumph Tiger Cub, which with its small thorax in relation to the wheels looks rather like a pesky insect.

'The Tiger Cub was the bike everyone learned to ride on,' explains GBC with maternal pride. 'If you broke down you left it in a ditch, went home and got another one.' But this one, you feel, would never be left in a ditch. She has, after all, practically given birth to it. 'I restored it from scrap,' she says, having taken it to bits, put it in a bath and scrubbed it down with de-greaser. 'They said, "You'll never get that back on the road." I said, yes I would.' And she did.

Bar a few car owners' clubs, motorcyclists are the only road users keeping alive that pioneering 1950s spirit of motoring, when a journey was an adventure to be planned for and enjoyed as a pleasure in itself. And classic bike owners are a specialised subspecies of the motorcycle brother- and sisterhood. GBC doesn't believe a motorbike should ever be covered in plastic, but she is prepared to live and let live. 'The camaraderie between modern and old riders is very healthy,' she says. 'They think we're crazy, riding these rickety old oil-spewing things. But they always wave at you.' And among classic bike owners there is a further subdivision, between 'polishers' and 'riders' – those who leave their special machine in the drive to cast admiring looks at from the kitchen window and those who get on the damn thing and make it go – with GBC firmly in the latter camp.

The cyclists of the 1950s who featured in *The 39 Steps* had already discovered the charms of The Trossachs from a saddle. And now this road, with its near one hundred tricky bends, is regarded by bikers – especially classic bikers – as one of the most thrilling recreational routes in Scotland.

'On old bikes it's absolutely cracking,' says GBC. 'Because you can't open up the throttle, there's no pressure to be a hero. And because you're laid back, you have time to look around – even though you have to watch out for corners.' As we did just now, when we nearly ran into her. She has now completed the adjustments to her Triumph and we promise not to tell any of her male colleagues that she had to make running repairs. 'Of course, if I break down it's another chance for them [men] to laugh at me – silly little girl! But it's all in good nature, she says, and with that she kick starts the Cub, and roars off into the mists and bends of the wild Duke's Pass, while the Bentley looks after her like a dowager at an urchin.

For the rest of the ride over the pass we squint into the headlights of oncoming bikes and are twice buffeted by the slipstream of overtaking machines as we keep in low gear all the way. Scott's descriptions of The Trossachs in *The Lady of the Lake* may have been overblown, but it is not hard to see what he was getting at, nor why tourists flocked here in the nineteenth century.

The Duke's Pass is a sampler of everything you might wish and expect to find in a classic Highland landscape – plenty of lochs glinting in the intermittent sunlight, a backdrop of mist-enshrouded mountains and dark and brooding conifer forests, flowers growing on the verges, cattle grazing in meadows, waterfalls, stone bridges over babbling burns, bracken and heather and more heather. There seems to be a consensus on the representative beauty of this road, the 1950s guidebooks all saying pretty much the same thing. 'The Trossachs have everything in miniature – towering mountains, peaceful valley scenes, tree-girt lochs, historic places set against a background of legend and romance,' reckoned Christopher Trent, the author of *Motoring Holidays in Britain*, in 1959. It feels timely at this point to be twenty-first-century William Gilpins for a minute here and consider just what it is that makes a landscape – as opposed to, say, a tower block – so pleasing on the eye and uplifting of the mood.

And, wouldn't you know it, an academic has beaten us to it. Dr David Simmons, a lecturer in the Department of Psychology at the University of Glasgow, specialises in visual perception and has developed a theory about humans' relationship to views and why we are magnetised towards certain vantage points in the landscape, where we dutifully say, 'Wow!' as we unzip our cameras. Humans, he says, like visual stimuli, enjoy seeing both things that are familiar and things that are new.

'Perhaps novelty and familiarity compete with each other when we are viewing natural scenes,' says Dr Simmons. 'Sometimes we are looking for a new, more dramatic view of something, but other times we simply wish to return to our old haunts. But maybe viewing a natural scene "live" provides a perfect combination of familiarity and novelty. In mountainous areas like the west Highlands of Scotland, the constantly changing weather adds drama and novelty to a scene that may have been visited many times before.' In addition, and intriguingly, views may satisfy an atavistic need for safety and defence. For in being presented with a panorama of hills, woods and valleys, the Stone Age part of our brains understands that somewhere among them will be the perfect place to make a camp – hidden away and defensible from predators and enemies and with a perfect signal for one's mobile phone. Gilpin, eat your heart out.

One thing that is hidden away on the Duke's Pass is evidence of industry. For, like so many landscapes we have seen in the course of these journeys, this landscape has been shaped by man's toil. Among the conifers to either side of the road are the remains of slate quarries, and a little railway that climbed up to service them. The scale of quarrying here bore no comparison with the operations in north Wales, but at the end of the nineteenth century the Aberfoyle quarries were producing 1.4 million slates a year and their claim to fame is that Aberfoyle slate was used for the billiard tables on the luxury liner *Queen Mary*, when she launched in 1936. The quarries closed in the fifties and their old workings, now overgrown and invisible, lie to either side of the road as we drop down a 1:10 incline on a series of switchbacks towards Aberfoyle – which, surprise surprise, calls itself 'Gateway to The Trossachs'.

We, however, are taking the back door out of The Trossachs proper, towards the wild places once ruled by 'the children of the mist', the fighting men of the MacGregor clan who would appear as if from nowhere and vanish without trace after relieving you of your cow or – if you were a hobbling peasant – pushing some guineas into your hand.

At the bottom of the Duke's Pass, rather than turning left into Aberfoyle – which has been described as more car park than town – we turn sharp right on to the B829 signposted to Inversnaid (15 miles). On sharp turns like this the long bonnet with its proud, winged B symbol at the prow behaves more like an oil tanker than a car, turning agonisingly slowly, but that is just the beginning of our worries. According to Trent in *Motoring Holidays in Britain*, 'One can drive from Aberfoyle to Inversnaid on a sunny Saturday afternoon in August without meeting more than two or three cars.' In our dreams. For the next hour – that's how long we'll take to reach Inversnaid – we make slow progress on the narrow, often single-track road and there will be frequent, humiliating stops to let our vehicular inferiors sneak past.

On the other hand, there's no hurry. And the scenery is terrific. Loch Ard presently appears on one side of the road, with a steep, forested hillside on the other. On the far bank of the loch there's a mix of broadleaf trees and conifers, the bare conifer trunks looking like clusters of toothpicks. We brush through tunnels of rhododendrons, past mossy stone walls and iron railings and a little shingle beach at Altskeith. Past Forest Hills Hotel and the hamlet of Kinlochard the road narrows further – barely room for those clockwork indicators to ping out – and a sign warns that we are approaching a single-track road with passing places. Wooden telegraph poles follow our route and a sign warns of falling rocks.

Beyond Loch Chon, the forestry plantations that have followed us practically all the way from Aberfoyle run out – and, refreshingly, we suddenly find ourselves driving through moorland and heather. Over to the left, the silver finger of Loch Arklet appears, its shores entirely bare of trees. It's a reminder of how the landscape once looked, but now the Forestry Commission has plans – opposed by some locals – to plant up Loch Arklet too. Red Robbo would doubtless sweep down in the night to smite the new growth with his broadsword.

It's best to proceed respectfully from now on, for we are entering the MacGregors' back yard. By the invigoratingly bleak eastern shore of Loch Arlet we turn right on to an unclassified road that takes us in five minutes to Stronachlachar Pier, near the western end of Loch Katrine. This modest place – a café that looks like an Edwardian railway station, a semi-circular pier with black and white iron railings, and a slipway – was a crucial point on the tourist trail.

Here, on the slipway to the left of the pier, is where the SS *Sir Walter Scott* was assembled in 1899. A little way inland – we passed it a couple of minutes ago on the way to the pier – is the Victorian gable-fronted building that used to be the Stronachlachar Hotel and is now private flats. An advertisement from 1891 commends the hotel as 'beautiful, highly-finished, commodious, and charmingly-situated' and stresses that 'During the Season Coaches run to and from Inversnaid, in connection with steamers on Loch Katrine and Loch Lomond'.

By the second half of the nineteenth century, tourists were being processed through The Trossachs with the efficiency of a sausage-making machine. They steamed up Loch Lomond, hopped off at Inversnaid, were taken by horse-drawn coach to Stronachlachar Pier, took the *Rob Roy* or the *Sir Walter* steam ship to Trossachs Pier – birthplace of Rob Roy, check; Ellen's Isle, check – and continued by road to Callander or Aberfoyle where they caught the train back home. Or they did it the other way round, anti-clockwise, starting with the rail terminals. Thus Stronachlachar once teemed with Victorian gents and ladies with their copies of *The Lady of the Lake*, and enterprising guides tugging at their sleeves to show them the sights – the spot where Liam Neeson's and Jessica Lange's characters would go on to have their Highland fling in the movie *Rob Roy*, for example.

Actually the places associated with Rob are real enough, despite being overlaid with so much humbug and haggis over the centuries. He was born in 1671 at Glen Gyle on the shore of Loch Katrine, to the north of us as we stand at Stronachlachar Pier. A Scottish king, Charles II, was on the throne when he was born, but as he grew up, the Stuarts were displaced by Germans from the House of Hanover, who regarded men who wore skirts and grew wild facial hair as dangerous heathens. The stage was set for a dramatic clash of cultures – and what a stage it was.

The MacGregors' lands around Loch Katrine, spreading west to the shores of Loch Lomond, were wildly romantic, albeit in a heathery way that probably made alfresco Highland flings rather scratchy, especially in a kilt (so don't believe everything you see in the film). They were also near the rich Lowland pastures, where cattle were ripe for the filching. The MacGregors made their living from cattle – moving them, protecting other people's in exchange for money (the origin of the term blackmail) and stealing them – especially from people who supported the Hanoverian king and Lowland laws.

232

So Rob grew up as a kind of Highland Del Boy, with his fingers in various, mostly beef, pies. We may not have heard of him were it not for the small matter of a grand that went missing during his dealings with the Duke of Montrose.

Montrose was the natural political enemy of the MacGregors – a Scots toff and supporter of the Act of Union of 1707, by which Scotland and England were united as one country under an English monarch. But he was prepared to do business with the Jacobite Rob Roy. MacGregor borrowed one thousand pounds from Montrose to buy Highland cattle, which he planned to sell at a profit in the Lowlands. The money was given by Montrose to MacGregor's drover – and neither dosh nor drover were seen again. Though Rob Roy offered to pay back the money as and when he could, he was declared an outlaw. Montrose's men destroyed his house at Inversnaid and are said to have raped and branded his wife. From this moment on, as he stalks the wild hills with revenge in his belly and broadsword in his hand, his life becomes a series of escapades – of capture, and escape, and tweaking Montrose's effete and powdered nose, with plenty of philanthropy towards the Duke's downtrodden tenants thrown in.

The small wooded island ahead as you stand on the pier at Stronachlachar is called Factor's Island and it is where Rob Roy held Montrose's rent collector, Grahame of Killearn, having relieved him of funds. Rob Roy died in 1734 at Balquhidder, a few miles north of Loch Katrine, and lies in the graveyard there. His headstone says

'MacGregor despite them'. Fourteen years after Rob Roy's death, at the bloody Battle of Culloden, Highland culture was destroyed for ever as a viable force.

Our journey finishes in the heart of Rob Roy country. Back we go to Loch Arklet on the unclassified road, and continue west along the shore of the loch, with the undulating peaks of the 'Arrochar Alps' – the mountains on the western side of Loch Lomond – filling our windscreen. We are in a high, hanging valley at this point. Beyond the end of the loch, the road plunges in a series of zigzags and the Bentley noses gingerly towards the deep glacial trench of Loch Lomond. The ancient trees around us – not a sitka spruce among them – are the remnants of oak woodland planted by the Duke of Montrose after he confiscated the lands from Rob Roy.

At the bottom we emerge by Loch Lomond as if into the lobby of a vast and dazzling hotel after a bumpy elevator ride. The sheer scale of Loch Lomond – 24 miles long, five miles wide at its widest, with the largest surface area of any lake in the UK – puts The Trossachs and its cosy little lochs and hills into perspective. The light reflecting off that vast surface area of water seems momentarily overwhelming. And so we park the Bentley with its iconic flying letter B pointed across the glittering silver waters at the western shore of heather-covered mountains, rising like a dark wall in the gathering dusk. Behind us are the Inversnaid Falls, funneling foaming peat-brown water many hundreds of feet down from Loch Arklet, and the Inversnaid Hotel, which would have been a busy place in its Victorian heyday. It is now owned by a coach company, but there are no coaches in the car park today. Just one car besides our own.

This is Inversnaid – a waterfall, a hotel and a pier, and a strangely hypnotic atmosphere. Two poets, in very different ways, have captured the spirit of Inversnaid. On his visit with his sister Dorothy and fellow poet Samuel Taylor Coleridge in 1803, William Wordsworth was dazzled by the pubescent charms of the Inversnaid ferryman's sister and wrote *To the Highland Girl of Inversnaid* to get it off his chest. Her beauty, he said, had turned the trees, the waterfall, the little bay and quiet road into 'something fashion'd in a dream'. He caught the ferry to the other side of Loch Lomond shortly before the vice squad turned up.

Seventy-eight years later, Gerard Manley Hopkins paid a flying visit. He wasn't on the tourist trail. He had no desire to declaim *The Lady of the Lake* from The Trossachs tops. In fact, two poets whose work was less alike than Scott and Hopkins would be hard to imagine. He simply wanted a break from Glasgow, where he was working at St Joseph's Church as a Jesuit priest. At the end of September 1881 he was given two days off to see the Highlands and hurried up to Loch Lomond. 'The day was dark and partly hid the lake, yet it did not altogether disfigure it but gave a pensive or solemn beauty which left a deep impression on me,' he wrote. At Inversnaid he walked by the waterfall and that day he wrote a short poem called *Inversnaid* with a famous verse that packs a modern message: 'What would the world be, once bereft/ Of wet and wildness? Let them be left/ O let them be left, wildness and wet/ Long live the weeds and the wilderness yet.'

He would be pleased to know that in the 130 years since he wrote those lines, the wildness and the wet have been left in this quiet place. We are at the end of the road. There is nowhere to go. A couple in cagoules, no doubt walking the West Highland Way, break stride to admire the Bentley before hurrying on. And all that one hears is the quiet ticking of the cooling engine.

Acknowledgements

We are indebted to the following: Brian Bennett, Chris and Jimmy Brown, Roger and Ruth Brown, Martin and Val Baker, Barbara Britton, Tony Bennett, Allen Buckley, Bob Crossley, Mike Edwards, Father Bischoi, Gorgeous Biker Chick, Mick Holder and Henry Mills, Bethan Gwanas, Martin Jackson, John and Gail Jennings, Derek Jones, Eric Jones, Dr Richard Jones, Mark Kibblewhite, Richard Leafe, James Lindsay, Victor Middleton, Ian Mitchell and William Jackson, Robin Morgan and Richard Daniels, Richard Motley, Hugh O'Neil, Rupert Pullee, Anne Rainsbury, Peter Walker, Tim Ryan, Dr David Simmons, Dr Ian Williams. Apologies for any inadvertent omissions.

Special thanks to Neil Edwards, Jonney Steven and Caroline Carmichael at Twofour Productions; Stuart

Cooper and Claire Potter at Metrostar Media; Gill Charlton for pushing the boat out; Juliana Foster for her excellent copy editing; Andrea Henry at Headline for making it possible; Miren Lopategui for all her patience and support.

Index of Place Names

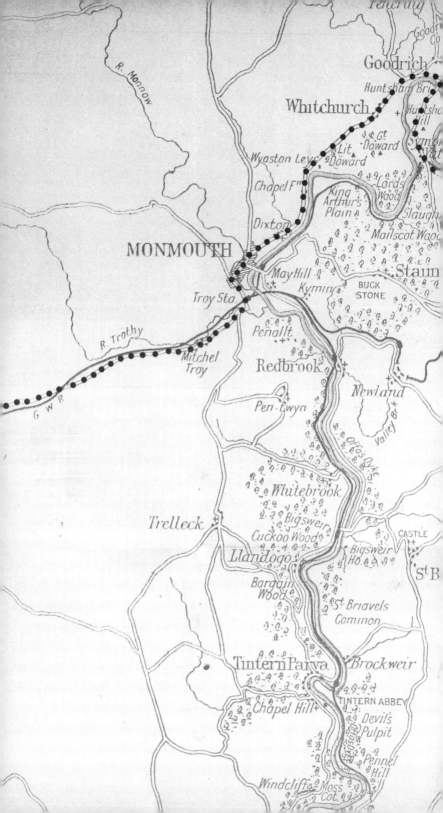